DHARMA

CORNERSTONE OF INDIAN CIVILIZATION

NIXON FERNANDO
nixfdo@gmail.com

Dharma: Cornerstone of Indian Civilization

Copyright © 2020 Nixon Fernando

All rights reserved.

ISBN:978-93-5408-137-8
This edition published 2020 by Nixon Fernando
No 10 Raman Nagar, Laxmipuram, Chennai
600099
www.nixonfernando.in

Typeset by: Kindle Direct Publishing
Printed and bound by: Kindle Direct Publishing
Visit
https://kdp.amazon.com/en_US/
for any further information

This book is dedicated to the fond memory of

SMT JAYALAKSHMI SESHAN

As representing the amazing women of India who are steeped in
tradition, who in accordance with their dharma live their lives as
anchors of the Family

CONTENTS

APPENDIX

PREFACE

The term 'Dharma' represents something invaluable, discovered to have amazing applicability and deployable in society to great impact. One needs to understand it for what it is, in order to benefit from its many graces. With this in mind, the book was designed to collect in one place important ideas regarding Dharma. The attempt has been to approach it from first principles, so that a person groomed in the scientific temperament can grasp the nuances and appreciate the beauty of the precept.

This book was conceived to act as a syllabus for a possible finishing school of Dharma and Leadership. Two earlier books, which the author co-authored, contained a few chapters on this topic. The ideas from these, and several articles written by him on the subject, have been put together to create a comprehensive book dedicated exclusively to Dharma.

Dharma, as an ideal, has been in vogue in the Indian Civilization for more than 5000 years and a lot could be written about it. But there is a need to filter out the non-essentials and present it in a complete, yet concise form that will make sense to even someone who is hard pressed for time. The compilation, therefore, needed to be handy and focused. Very importantly, it had to be presented in a way that someone educated in the present era could comprehend easily. Some minimal repetition has been used, in the interest of ensuring completeness of chapters.

Indians, more often than not, get it when they are told to do their dharma. This is owing to the ingenious institution of informal education that is part of Indian tradition, which includes story telling or play acting themes from the Puranas as a part and parcel of community and family life. When themes from the Puranas are enacted, wisdom seeps into the audience. However, an informal system can misfire, with inaccurate communication resulting in wrong concepts being propagated. As such, the confusion that exists today is natural and it needs to be addressed. People can either know about Dharma through instinct, or from being trained in the skill, or know it in-depth through understanding of its nuances. These are different things and only in the last case (through understanding) can one be confident, without an iota of doubt, in taking decisions and in demonstrating leadership that is tuned to excellence always. An attempt, therefore, needs to be made to resolve the technicalities involved so that one knows, by understanding, what Dharma is and be clear about acting in accordance with it.

This clarity is of immense value in the context of one being able to distinguish between genuine and fraudulent use. The word Guru, for instance, holds a very specific meaning in the Scriptural context; but today, all and sundry having anything to teach or communicate are casually referred to as Guru. This is actually sacrilege, but nothing can be done about it apart from throwing light on the actual meaning. The same thing applies to 'Dharma' as well. For example a thief claims that his Dharma is to steal and feed his family. So he says a prayer in a house of worship—that he should be able to steal well that day, and then sets out to steal. He takes comfort from the fact that he has been able to define thieving as his 'Dharma'. Now that is a total mockery of the term and the truth is that people do this indiscriminately today. Even murder is being committed and condoned in the name of Dharma.

No wonder then that there is such degradation of public life in India. The anchor, on which righteous action was hinged, is now no longer connected to its true moorings. Pretty much any amorous act is condoned in public life and it is difficult to distinguish who is righteous and who is not. It has badly affected values in public life.

This failure to clear the confusion partially comes from the fact that the term Dharma is considered part of Hindu Religion and is therefore kept out of 'secular' Indian public life. This has even kept the term out of genuine academic research. The truth about Dharma though, is that it is a secular principle. It should be a part of normal life in India even in an official sense.

The intention of this book therefore, is to lead a discussion on this concept that is vital to the learning and traditions in the land were the Sindu flows. The claim is that the pursuit of Dharma can change lives. It can help one do their duties with pleasure, live fearlessly in faith, live in harmony with society, live inspired and above all find contentment and satisfaction in life. It is an 'application' built out of the 'greatest treasure known to man'. It can help build individual merit and it can give prosperity to individuals, families, castes, communities, societies and nations.

ACKNOWLEDGMENT

I thank Mr. Seshan for having trusted me with this work, having extended useful support, given direction and provided opportunities to make this possible. He has also been immensely kind in giving a thoughtful foreword.

Thanks also to prof. Bala V Balachander who is one of the authors of the book 'Yogyathwa' along with Mr. Seshan and I. Some of the important ideas related to Dharma have been taken from this book.

Thanks are also due to Dr. Bala Krishna, Dr. Shiviling Hullavard, Ms. Neha Hiremath, Mr. RK Ramanathan, Ms. Rohini Joshi, Ms. Jayashree Hiremath, Col Vinay Dalvi and Ms. Annam Anandan, Mr. RH Raghavan and Mr. BV Rao for their valuable initial feedback that has helped in improving the contents.

I have no words to express my deep gratitude to my brother Sabas Fernando who did immense amount of work to make this book readable. Besides correcting the language flow he has offered valuable inputs to improve the contents.

Thanks also to Janet Fernando for designing the cover of the book.

And most of all, thanks to Amazon for having provided the platform to have this book published.

FOREWORD

Despite the prevailing despondency in the Indian nation, I have always nurtured, and sill nurture, a fond hope within me that the ancient learning of ours will re-assert itself and the sub-continent will once again rise to peace and prosperity. The civilization has withstood crises for many thousands of years and it will withstand the present onslaught too. All it will take for a nation to rise, is for its leaders to perform their duties with discipline and dignity. Dharma should be in fashion yet again and we would have arrived. But I still ask myself how does one get there?

It gives me pleasure to forward this book because it points in a direction of promise. If India must rise, it must ask deep questions and introspect. This book does ask and answer some of those questions. The author makes a strong case for us to re-visit our understanding of past wisdom and he focuses on 'Dharma' which he says, and I agree, is the most important thing in the Indian Civilization.

The author: Nixon was one of the senior students of the second batch of the MIT School of Government that we set up at Pune with the intention of grooming future leaders. He came to me in

Chennai in 2007 in connection with research about my work at the Election Commission and has been associated with me ever since. After the passing away of my wife, he spends most of his time with me doing research and helping me with my intellectual work.

He has done well in his academics, in his extracurricular activities and in his service life at the NDA, and he also has an MBA to boot. So I even asked him one day, 'What are you doing here?'

He has been into a deep study of the Indian situation and has been researching solutions for more than 25 years now. He told me, "When you were cleaning up the commission and your popularity rivaled the best of Bollywood stars, I was just out of university watching and hoping one day I would be able to present to you my ideas on how we could solve the problems of the nation. Destiny has brought me to your home". Of late he has been asking me questions on what must be done in various areas in Indian society and Government and has been compiling the answers.

Nixon has written several books in the area of his research; the latest one being a huge compendium which he calls a Vision for India entitled "Rising to Second freedom". He has written a book on the farmers' suicides in Vidarbha. And he even did the leg work for the book 'Yogyathwa: Simple Access to Powerful Leadership" by Dr Bala Balachander and myself and he is one of the co-authors.

The right person for this book: I had asked him to work on the possibility of setting up of a finishing school that taught about Leadership and Dharma. This book is an outcome of that. What has emerged is a useful narrative on Dharma; and one can understand why it is of great importance to India.

He is the right person for writing this book because he has the acumen and has intensely studied select scriptures, especially the Bhagwad Gita. His unique perspective on the Hindu system of thought is both meaningful and one that easily blends with the teachings of his own Christian faith and the teachings of other religions. Through such a universal perspective, he brings out hidden gems of wisdom that give us opportunities to introspect. Also, for Nixon, firm grounding in rational thought comes through his post-graduation in Physics and yet he sees no conflict between science and spirituality. Therefore, this perspective that sees resonance in the various religions, in science and in the works of the likes of Mahatma Gandhi is invaluable; it will help in the search for harmony in today's public thought

A Brief Synopsis: I had advised him to begin the book with a chapter dedicated to debunking the idea that Dharma is equivalent of Religion. He has done that. Dharma is indeed not religion. Dharma is above religion as it universally applies to all of humanity and it deals with every act and interaction of each individual. Chapter 3 has a perspective on four things that impel action in human beings: Kama, Artha, Dharma and Moksha. Nixon's analysis of this age old model shows that people who acknowledge only the first two of these as realities of human existence live lesser lives compared to those who know instinctively (or otherwise) that there are four.

Chapter 4 is the one that takes the reader back to basics. I always hold the view that "Dharma IS"; it is an experience and no amount of word power is going to do justice to describing it. But Dharma also manifests in society and Nixon has picked up four aspects of it and has been able to elaborate on the idea in a way that the insight will help in understanding and applying Dharma. Obedience to the will of the Supreme, establishment of the rule of law, transition from duty to no duty and the time and place specificity of a given Dharma are all important aspects of Dharma.

But Chapter 8 is by far the most crucial of the chapters in the book. In it, the author answers the question, "If Lord Rama was alive today, what is the systemic Dharma he would follow and protect?"

Taking it up from the first principles discussed earlier in the book, Nixon argues how 'Democracy' is the Dharmic solution that has been arrived at as the best possible in the present era. It has been recommended by leading lights of the world. The Indian elders too have chosen democracy and have established the Constitution of India as the mother document that tells us how team India will work together through democracy. Just as Arjuna was asked to defend the monarchic Dharma of his age, the citizens of today's India are called upon to defend the democracy set up under the Constitution of India—Indians have to stand by the Constitution and take the nation to greater heights.

He remarks: "It is not ok if someone steals and murders out in the world and comes to a temple or church or mosque and offers a 'cut' as donation to God." He implies that working for the Constitution is as sacred as is working for a house of worship.

The book then winds up with two chapters dedicated to how each individual must find what his role in the modern Dharma is, how he can excel in his duties, and how the pursuit of Dharma alone is going to give him satisfaction of a life truly lived.

What is of value in the book and to whom is it relevant: This is not a very large book but it is deep. It addresses the questions related to contentment in life and finding meaning in what one does. It attempts to restore to the limelight something that was a core motivating principle of the civilization. And surely it will provoke the readers to re-visit values, take reference with respect to some of the greatest ideas known to man and begin each day with better assurance that one is making his way after understanding what the wise want from him—in pursuit of the highest joy recommended by the ancients.

It is a must read for the Hindu, for the teacher, for the leader—in fact for every thinking individual; because of the universality of Dharma. An understanding of Dharma—and more importantly its experience—shows a pathway to calm down in the present intellectual noise and move forward assured that one is acting in resonance with the Supreme Spirit. At a time when the world has to deal with impending crises of environment, poverty and annihilation, the din in the public discourse is not helping. It is now time for timeless and universal thoughts like Dharma to re-surface and lead humanity to better places. Therefore this book is both significant and timely

An important part of the book is that there is no brow beating. It is an exposition with which a reader is free to agree, or disagree. And for those averse to Metaphysical references, Nixon offers rational practical suggestions all along, which throw light on best suggested practices that both make sense and are in harmony with Dharma; so even those that do not have faith can benefit. It is self-education, if one adds this awareness to himself, of an idea that has been cherished for five thousand years or more. For all we know, it may light up the spark that sets real leaders going.

What this means to me: Duty has always been close to my heart, but Dharma is closer. Duty with Discipline and Dignity is Dharma. I have been groomed to stand up for what is righteous and I am proud to say that I did not relent for anything or anybody in all my service life. In the beginning of my career, at my very first independent posting, I had run into trouble with two Tamil Nadu ministers over a punishment I gave to a fourth person, someone important to the ministers; but the fellow was caught with his hand in the till. I went by the rule book and did not compromise to please anyone. Angry, the ministers offloaded me from their car in the middle of nowhere, in the hot sun and drove off. Chief Minister Kamaraj was gracious and righteous enough to stand by me and chided the ministers in my presence and that too in public. And so on, till when I was Cabinet Secretary, when I took drastic steps for Government to function on a day the entire opposition was on strike—as per the legitimate orders of the Prime Minister; on all occasions the rule of law was never compromised. And that was, in other words, upholding of the Constitution, which, in turn, Nixon shows, is nothing but the upholding of Dharma.

My work at the Election Commission can be summarized as just that; restoring the constitutional status of the Election Commission of India. Before I took office there was a time the Chief Election Commissioner sat in the waiting room of the Law Minister seeking to have expenses for the purchase of some books cleared. The impression was that the Election Commission was an appendage of the Law Ministry. I would have none of it. The Constitution wanted the Election Commission to be an autonomous body answerable to the parliament under certain conditions. On how the elections were to be conducted on ground the CEC was to be final authority. The governments on the other hand wanted the Commission to be pliant to their needs. I had to rage a tough battle to pull the Election Commission free from the Government's clutches. Can you imagine that the person responsible for elections in the biggest democracy of the world stopped all election related work? It happened; in August 1993. For ten days all hell broke loose. When the then Supreme Court recognized that there was merit in my claim, it gave an order in my favor and I revoked my orders and elections were on once again. Whether it was asking governments to issue voter ID's to all voters or whether it was implementing the Model Code of Conduct, or issuing show cause notices to a whole lot of Rajya Sabha MPs for wrongly stating their place of residence, everything was done keeping the rule of law paramount and upholding the Constitution at all times. I would quote rules and laws in all my decisions.

Now why am I telling all this here? It is because when the sincere government official way down the line understands that the systems operate according to the rule-of-law, then you see lions rise up amongst them. There were instances of DM's switching off power supply to Union Ministers' microphones exactly at 10.00PM, a sub inspector stopping a notorious MP from entering a constituency and registrars reporting on Union Ministers for forgery. When they know that the rule of law prevails—that the constitutional Dharma is being implemented from up above, they do their jobs diligently. The same government mechanism that was responsible for governance under the government, which did not seem to be too happy doing government work, would deliver comfortably on the election front. Holding up Dharma at the highest level adds great energy to any togetherness. In contrast, ego driven systems create confusion, despondency and fear in people. In Dharma alone the Nation can rise to Greatness.

In conclusion: If as a teacher you want to deliver the best to your students, do please understand the nuances of Dharma and enlighten your students, it can transform their lives. If you are a leader in any capacity, the principle of Dharma will add great strength to you and your organization. And even if you are just a citizen taking care of any kind of responsibility in society, if you stand by Dharma you stand focused on the way to Moksha. This book is sure to set you thinking along the right directions.

I have one wish for you, the same gift that Lord Rama's mother gave her son when he set out on exile: "The Dharma that you protect will protect you".

Bless you all.

Jai Hind!

TN Seshan, IAS (Retd)
Former Chief Election Commissioner of India
Chennai,
18/10/2019

INTRODUCTION

By the dharma is meant the heart, for there is no dharma apart from the heart.
----Huangbo Xiyun

A nation famed for its wisdom, its insight on human beings and its spiritual depth, India is still languishing among the least nations of the world on scales relating to many dimensions of human development including mortality rates, poverty rates, disease rates, illiteracy and many others. The solutions, which the powers that be are working at, barely show a flicker of light at the end of the tunnel. Caste and communal issues rule the roost. The family, as a building block of society seems under threat. Corruption is often perceived in society as the norm. Is this the best that India can be? Are we missing something? Do we have potential for better? If we do, then what is it that can unleash that potential?

Is Dharma the correction?

The term 'Dharma' holds great significance in the thought process of Indian civilization. Consider the following: The Om, The One, The Highest and The Purusha, are terms used to refer to the 'Highest Principle' which the Vedas propound. This 'Highest Principle' is represented in the Puranas in the Trimurthy or Brahma, Vishnu and Maheshwara. Each one represents that principle completely. Vishnu manifests in the role of preserver. The 'basic role' of this manifestation of the Highest Principle—we can even call it the 'only' role of this manifestation of the Highest Principle—is the 'establishment of Dharma'. Lord Rama's upholding of Dharma is the central theme of the Ramayana. In the same manner, Lord Krishna's role in the Mahabharata is exclusively about the establishment of Dharma. Verses 4:7&8 in the Bhagwad Gita eloquently state:

"Whenever, O descendant of Bharata, there is decline of Dharma, and rise of Adharma, then I body myself forth.

For the protection of the virtuous, for the destruction of the wicked, and for the establishment of Dharma, I come into being in every age."

Therefore, the task assigned to the Highest Principle known to the Indian civilization, is the setting up of 'Dharma'. The sense of how important this is, is best grasped from what Jesus Christ says about the 'Kingdom of heaven':

"Again, the kingdom of heaven is like a merchant seeking fine pearls, and upon finding one pearl of great value, he went and sold all that he had and bought it." Bible, Matthew 13:45-46

The phrase 'The kingdom of Heaven' is equivalent to the Indian concept of 'Ramrajya'. As such it is about the 'outcome of work in the world' of the Highest Power, not a description of The Highest Power itself. Even so, this verse indicates the same relevant scale of priority; and the highest point along the scale is the subject of discussion here.

Dharma is therefore about manifesting the work of that Highest

Principle known to the Indian sages. It is hence one of the centerpieces in Indian Spirituality. If Dharma, as a concept, did not exist, there was no purpose for Lord Krishna in the Mahabharata. It is also a fact that the human-hero of this epic (Arjuna) is celebrated because he rises to fight for Dharma.

Just as Arjuna went on to play his Dharmic role in society, it is tradition and practice in Indian system, that each person is expected to raise their level of consciousness and perform Dharma. Dharma is therefore the prime instrument for motivation in the traditional system that prevails in the sub-continent. It is at the very heart of the great tradition of spiritual learning which has been passed down through the millennia.

In terms of Christian Theology: In Christian theology, it is said that 'the word was made flesh in Jesus Christ'; the 'word' being the word of God. The central prayer in the Christian faith, taught by Jesus Christ himself, 'The Our Father', has this expression: 'Thy will be done on Earth'. The faithful pray here, that God's will may be done -by the system, by people in general and also by themselves. Jesus Christ also tells his followers 'give up yourself, take up your cross, and follow me'; meaning that his followers are to obey the Father's expectations just as Jesus Christ obeyed—even if it is a call unto death. 'The Father' is the highest principle as far as Christianity is concerned. The 'word of God', 'Thy will be done', 'give up yourself…' are all core principles of the Christian faith and they vastly imply, by equivalence, a call to dharma (we shall see the specifics eventually).

Buddhism: The Buddhist tradition calls for upholding of Dhammam. Three of the anchor principles of the Buddhist faith are The Buddha, Dhammam and the Sangam (brotherhood). Dhammam entails the same essence in equivalence of Dharma. Even though the use of a Supreme Being and Supreme Self is not part of the Buddhist faith, the sense delivered by Dhammam is indeed the same as Dharma and it is a central principle to

Buddhists.

Islam: In Islam, like in Hinduism and Christianity, there is reference to the Highest Power and 'His' will. Again, obedience to this Highest Power is considered as Jihad in its purest form. The Holy Quran offers that guidance on what that Supreme Will wants from the followers of Islam. With the following of the Quran considered central to Islam, great stress is placed on a principle that is equivalent to Dharma in substance.

The equivalence of the term Dharma with these concepts from the other religions will unravel as we go into the details later on. For now, however, we must take note that the principle of Dharma and its equivalents are centrally placed in the practice of these faiths.

Ignoring such a principle only invites peril.

When we talk of morality and value systems today, there seems to be a gaping hole; having a value system without an equivalent of 'Dharma' in place, seems rather naïve especially when such high importance is given in the various faiths of the world. In a place like India, whose traditions thrive on Dharma, ignoring it in our attempts to build values does not seem logical.

Going even further spiritual literature indicates that such selfless obedience to the highest power, as required by Dharma, resonates with the highest potential of humans. Remarkable research by Maslow in the area of transcendental psychology (when he was nearing the end of his life) points in the same direction. People who diligently stand by Dharma are known to be excellent at what they do. The recommendation from both sources is that one must aim to realize his highest potential, as in this alone can one achieve completeness. Therefore if Dharma ensures this, (we shall presently see how this is connected) how can one ever slight the study of this promising ideal?

Most value systems present the yen for righteousness as the all-important struggle between good and evil. The Hindus paraphrase it as a struggle between Dharma and Adharma. With the Godhead, in Hindu scriptures, being occupied with Dharma, it is ample indication that the wise men of ancient India have found that it is through Dharma alone that any civilization can rise to maximize its potential. It is not sensible to ignore an ideal like dharma.

A word of caution for those who practice Dharma through their traditions: There is a systemic aspect to Dharma and an individual aspect to it. Dharma is about setting up of a righteous system, but it is also about each individual pursuing a certain discipline. Those who practice Dharma at their individual level may find the reflections about Dharma long winded and elaborate. But such yogis must realize that this study is an exercise in Gyan Yoga. Patience is advised. When one understands how the whole thing works, it will give reason to pursue their present Dharma with greater vigor.

CHAPTER 1
THE WORD DHARMA IS NOT SYNONYMOUS WITH RELIGION

Dharma is a Sanskrit word. It simply means that which is right, that which is correct, that which is the divine law.

----Frederick Lenz

Google reports that the word 'set' has 464 different meanings officially recognized in the Oxford Dictionary. Besides these, there can be many more because each individual mind can add its own color to the meaning of a word owing to variations in perception. This multiplicity of meanings of words is therefore a matter of fact in language and in the science of perception.

Multiple meanings can lead to confusion. When the reader/listener is not in sync with the author's/speaker's understanding/usage of words then what gets communicated is—most of the time—a distortion of the original message. The ambiguity, which can be either accidentally or wantonly created, is immense.

What then, does the term 'Dharma' really mean?

The wise who have written the scriptures had a meaning associated to the term 'Dharma' and the attempt in the book, will be to unravel that meaning to the exclusion of distortions. While subsequent chapters deal with the real meaning of the word 'Dharma', this chapter is dedicated to refute the perception that Dharma is same as Religion, which it is not.

Very often, we hear the term 'Dharma' used in the following manner, "He belongs to the Hindu Dharma" or "He belongs to the Christian Dharma". Here 'Dharma' is used as a substitute for the term Religion. When used in this sense, the injunction to be Dharmic would mean that somebody who belongs to the Christian religion should be dogmatic in the pursuit of his faith. This elaboration of the term is incorrect. To be 'Dharmic' does not necessarily mean that one must be dogmatic in his religious beliefs. Yet the pursuit of faith is recommended in Dharma.

Religion, both in its constitution and practice needs to be Dharmic. Building clarity step-wise, let us initially consider this word to initially mean 'righteous'. Yet still, religion in its practice, is often not up to the mark. The opposite of Dharma is Adharma. One notes that many aspects of the pursuit of a religion may be Dharmic, but some seem to fall in the realm of Adharmic. Each religion can be assessed to be Dharmaic or Adharmic in parts depending on how it is being practiced. In that sense, one can see that Dharma is more elementary and universal as a principle, in comparison to religion.

A complexity of religion is revealed in this statement by Mahatma Gandhi: "There are as many religions, as there are people in this world". The meaning being, that the practice of a certain 'spiritual discipline' - which one may define as 'religion' – differs from person to person. For example, even within a family, a father is regular in his prayers at the home altar, while his son does not say his daily prayers but visits a nearby temple once in a while, unlike his father. The same religion, same caste, same family and yet, the practice is different. What works for the father, the father pursues and what the son sees as necessary and proper, the son pursues. This is true about all great religions of the world. While there can be a standardized prescription for being ideal followers, it is not necessary that what manifests in the minds of the followers is identical. For each individual, the religion manifests differently. Incidentally, this difference does, in one way, take the definition of religion closer to the term 'Dharma'—because 'Dharma' has an element of what the divine has ordained for each person individually. For example, Christ was called to have a physical death after torture and after being nailed on to a cross - that was what Dharma demanded of him. The demands of the Supreme on Guru Arjan Dev Singh, Meera Bai, Akkamahadevi or on Ramana Maharishi were different.

Religion is what one practices out of their belief, while Dharma is that which one 'ought to do' out of obedience to the Supreme Self (this is elaborated further in chapter 4). As such, asking a person to uphold dharma is not identical with asking him to practice precisely what he perceives the priestly class has defined for him as religion. Yet if the religion is true, and if in practice, it is in consonance with essential spirituality, then the pursuit of Dharma for an individual will find resonance in the pursuit of that religion.

If we pause for a moment and look at the relationship between the concepts we have been considering, it would be clear that Religion is a sub-set – and Dharma is the whole. Religion is essentially an attempted manifestation of the ideal of Dharma. Religion, in its purest form is one aspect of Dharma. Dharma is a secular principle and applies uniformly to all true religions.

Another term in common usage is "Sanathana Dharma". People often use it interchangeably with "Dharma". Assuming this equivalence is erroneous.

There is variation in the definition of what Sanathana Dharma actually means and different scholars approach it differently. The term 'Sanathana,' in Sanskrit, means 'original' or as 'eternal'. However the term "Sanathana Dharma", as a phrase, does not carry that idea.

To begin with, Sanathana Dharma has an element of exclusivity in it. A large portion of those considered Hindus, are classified as 'avarna'- those who do not belong to the 'varna' system. In other words, they are not integral to the core of Hinduism consisting of the Varanachala Dharma or Sanathana Dharma. With exclusivity being a characteristic by definition, 'Sanatana Dharma' ceases to be the eternal-universal while Dharma on the other hand is known to be universal.

The exclusion of the avarnas from the "Sanathana Dharma", in truth, makes Sanathana Dharma only a sub set of Hinduism. So "Sanathana Dharma" and "Hindu Dharma" themselves are not equivalent in the first place.

Sanathana Dharma also has political, social, spiritual and economical dimensions in its constitution. As such, since it is all inclusive, it does constitute a Dharma (This will be taken up in Chapter 4). However, it cannot be equated to a religion as defined in contemporary literature. It seeks to define a way of life and so in modern terms – it is more than a religion. Consequently, 'Sanatana Dharma', though only a smaller part of Hinduism, by itself it covers more space than a religion would.

A critical consideration is that if Sanathana Dharma stands strongly by its political and economic dimensions, embracing them as integral to it, it should be caught in a time warp. An appeal to uphold Sanathana Dharma would then call for some Hindus to trace back their ancestry, find out the caste to which they are supposed to belong, and then take up the responsibilities of that caste. This would include an attempt to uphold monarchy during the times of Democracy. This would not make sense. Political, social and economic systems have changed over the centuries, largely because of science and technology. What we have today is a radically changed environment. Sanathana Dharma/varnachala

Dharma, defined for an age when society was relatively low tech and when the most efficient system of government was monarchy, ceases to be relevant in that form today. Indeed, if Sanathana Dharma is to be interpreted as standing for something eternal, the socio-political-economic aspects should not be a part of it; Sanathana Dharma cannot be eternal or universal if it is. The only alternative left is that Sanathana Dharma should have both fixed and variable features in it. It would then, through its variable aspect, adapt itself to match today's needs. It must re-cast the variable aspect in its constitution (Smriti) in order to suit the present times, and it must do so without meddling with that which is fixed and eternal (Shruti). Review and re-adjustment of "Sanathana Dharma" is in any case imminent.

Therefore, if there is non-inclusion in "Sanathna Dharma" and if it is rigidly fixed in the definition of its political and economic aspect – it is limited in its reach. This makes it different from 'Dharma', which on the other hand, is known to be something universal and relevant at all times.

In summary, Dharma is not synonymous with the Religion. As such, the use of the term Hindu Dharma or Islamic Dharma is not accurate. A true religion is only a subset of Dharma. As for Sanathana Dharma, in the form that it is practiced, it represents a Dharma for a certain time and age and needs adjustment of its time and place specific aspect to suit a new age.

CHAPTER 2

IDEALS ARE INDISPENSABLE. WHY NOT DHARMA?

Today people live to work rather than work for a living. They have forgotten their true goal in life. Subsequently they have forgotten their dharma. There is no communication between hearts, there is no sharing. Having lost contact with other's hearts, we become totally isolated. But in truth we are not isolated islands, we are links that form one chain.

----Mata Amritanandamayi

Ideals are a reality of human existence:

One cannot really draw a line. A line is defined as a locus of points and points have no width. Anything representing a straight line, drawn anywhere will have some thickness; it is in truth, not a line! Does that mean that a 'line' drawn has no use at all? In the same manner, one must not get entangled in a debate of idealism Vs practicality; ideals play a vital role in practical life. Just as is the case in the material sciences, so also it is in the social sciences.

Practical team work happens best with idealistic principles offering a guiding light. No team work can happen without shared ideals or vision. When operating in teams, whatever be the level, ideals are indispensable. For example the ideal of 'freedom' made the Americans fight their struggle for freedom. Another ideal of freedom made the French revolution happen. Ideals even guide our mutual interactions and our social actions. These ideals are agreed upon formally or informally and either overtly or subtly. These ideals form part of what is identified as 'social contract' - a nature of agreement humans make with society. Civilizations emerge when humans learn to live together - and shared ideals are contained in the reasoning behind almost everything in that civilization.

Conversely, since societies, communities, nations and such other groupings are a reality of today, it implies that they must be sharing ideas/ideals amongst themselves. These shared ideals are not a constant over time and place. Some nations want kingship instead of democracy; some individuals in India also think dictatorship should be is the order of the day for India. Some nations that wanted kingship once upon a time, now want democracy. Strong examples of shared ideals, at work teams, abound: be it Science, Secularism, Rule of Law, Affirmative Action, Human Rights, Monarchy, Democracy, Capitalism, Communism, Patriarchy, Welfare State and so on. The selection of good ideals matters to the prosperity of such teams. Going by the relative success in the material plane attained by some of the leading nations of the world, the present civilization seems to have zeroed in on ideals like Democracy, Capitalism, Human Rights, Statehood, Freedom, United Nations' principles, rule of law etc. as the preferred set of ideas for its cohesive pursuit… It is on the basis of these ideals and ideas that people relate to each other and take team decisions.

It is indeed clear, that ideas/ideals do exist and they are knowingly or unknowingly used in today's societies and teams to good effect. The question is not really about whether or not to use ideals - it is about 'which set of ideals' we choose to use.

Can Dharma be such an ideal?

Since ideals are a part and parcel of human existence, the proposed use of the concept of Dharma need not be seen as a forced implant into a vacuum of ideas/ideals. Rather, it needs to be seen as an articulation of an alternate set of ideas, on the basis of which the cohesive pursuit can be shared.

Dharma and its equivalents are a set of ideals that are in use for thousands of years now and it has the recommendation of the wise. What remains to be seen, is how it fits into the scheme of ideals that already prevail in modern society. Does it dovetail into the concepts that are acknowledged today, or does it ask for a complete re-haul of the present idealism. Is Dharma an ideal emerging from a higher level of comprehension or is it taking us backwards? Calling to mind Einstein's observation: "A problem cannot be solved at the same level of consciousness that created it," does Dharma serve to raise the level of consciousness? Last but not the least, does it come into conflict with the ideal of 'separation of state from religion' that is integral to modern democracy? Dharma, therefore needs to be tested as an idea/ideal suitable for today.

How does one do that?

In science, it is well established that a more advanced theory does a better job at prediction and at building of relevant applications. Dharma, must withstand these tests too. It therefore remains to be seen whether the set of ideas encompassing Dharma does indeed lead to superior and refined pursuit of individual and team goals of peace, prosperity and happiness.

A leader must aim for excellence: Everyone gets a call to leaddhip at some or the other level. Leadership is a profound responsibility. Leaders get to make decisions for a team. They have followers walking in the path of their guidance. They have the opportunity to influence minds due to the vintage point they hold in social order. They have a say in designing systems that coordinate the efforts of everyone in the team. This being the case, leaders need to act, in accordance to what they believe is the best course of action known to man. Therefore, the challenge before the leader in the context of this book is this: when the leader has the opportunity to encourage his citizens to pursue an idea or an ideal, should he promote the pursuit of Dharma? Should he take decisions keeping in mind the ideas propounded in Dharma?

If an idea turns out to be really impressive and can deliver the optimum or the best results – why not? If Dharma fits the bill, then why should a leader not pursue it?

There are valid reasons to believe that, the depth of understanding of human nature in the concepts governing Dharma, is indeed far more advanced than in the understanding generated by modern day philosophers, psychologists, mind scientists and brain scientists. This hypothesis, of course needs testing and validation.

While being scientific in our approach, let us, at the least, not be prejudiced against the ancient thinking process. Let us not presume that the people of this time and age think more benevolently and more intelligently (for solutions) than anyone else in the entire human history.

The indications are that the pursuit of Dharma does indeed show great promise for addressing issues that beset humans of this age.

3 ADDRESS THE DHARMA IMPELLER FOR CONTENTMENT?

Four purusharthas or goals of the life be, So very crystal clear in life undisputedly;
Artha – getting useful wealth and prosperity, Finding the meaning for living herein truly;
Kama – fulfilling desires, acting repeatedly, It the physical, material desire fulfillment be;
Dharma – the foundation of all human goals be, Refers to obligations, conduct, moral duties;
Moksha – the liberation from the web of maya be, Freedom from the cycles of birth and death clearly;

— Munindra Misra, Goals of Life

The ancients had an interesting model about human nature, with Dharma integral to it. This model has components representing both the physical and meta-physical nature of man. This four 'Purusharths' model (Purush+Artha: spirit in humans + meaning; what holds meaning to the Spirit in humans), which for our convenience we will call the 'four-impeller model', is one of the important models that was used and institutionalized in ancient Indian society. Besides being a tool for learning, it was also a tool for broad based transfer of wisdom and technique, and a facilitator for excellence in society.

This model consists of recognizing four impellers that make people take to action. These are known by the terms Dharma, Artha, Kama and Moksha. Let us understand each one, not necessarily in any particular order of importance, but sequencing them from the familiar to the unfamiliar.

Kama: Humans respond to kama urges. The term signifies the urges/needs of the gross material body. It could be thirst, hunger, the feeling of cold, windiness, touch, fever… all such urges experienced on the body, which are capable of generating a response from humans. 'Kama' thus becomes an impeller for action. The common tendency is to equate this term to sensuousness. Though sensuousness is a part of it, the meaning of the word covers a wider sweep and encompasses the entire range of physical sensations experienced by the gross body.

Artha: This impeller has to do with attaining things that have 'meaning' for an individual's standing: Wealth, status, property, degrees, security and position are examples. It represents a pursuit of material welfare targeting the satisfaction of the mind—of things that could augment the individual identity in its interactions in society.

Dharma: This can best be introduced here as being related to the upholding of the 'rule of law'. It relates to the sense of showing fairness and justice to everyone. Dharma signifies that pursuit of individuals, which has to do with the welfare of others out of selfless motives (I do good unto him, not because he is related to me… but because he is another human being and deserves to be treated the way I would want myself to be treated). It is about empathy (what in Sanskrit would be called Sahanubhooti—saha-together, anubhuti-experiencing; experiencing along with), as though the other was none but oneself. Dharma also entails one's dutiful participation in a benevolent collective process that upholds the society in truth and righteousness. Therefore, this sense of 'dharma' and wanting to uphold justice impels an individual into action just as Kama & Artha do.

Moksha: An accepted truism is that everything that man does is related to the search for happiness. There is this impulse – the need for happiness – that keeps him going through life. Depending on their understanding of where happiness is available, people pursue it in a variety of things. People who believe happiness lies in amassing possessions diligently pursue exactly that. People who feel that satisfaction comes from lazing around, will do that. People who think singing songs brings them happiness will try to sing whenever they can. There is a rarer group of humans who, having being pointed in a different direction - that highest happiness lies 'in their true spiritual nature,' think and behave differently. Armed with knowledge that true human nature can only be experienced beyond a maze/illusion which has been created by the mind, they first engage in practices that help their minds quiet down. Once alerted to the true nature of the impulse of Moksha, they invest this effort, into finding their highest nature - the pursuit of everlasting life; for finding heaven-on-earth. Having themselves sensed the value (like the rare pearl), such people pursue moksha with deliberate intent. Alternatively, placing great trust in the beauty and goodness of the wise, they act out of faith in a wise man's guidance. After all, the Bible says 'the good are the light in the darkness of the righteous'

It is critical to note that 'Moksha' is not 'Salvation' the way it is perceived in western literature. Moksha is also not an escape from an existing un-desirable situation called 'life'. Moksha has to do with currently experiencing 'Everlasting Life' as recommended by Jesus Christ; it is about NOW, how a person, who has 'transcended' his ego and individuality, lives a life of a hero— celebrating the present moment.

How the Purusharths model applies: – The Purusharths model considers all four - Kama , Artha, Dharma, Moksha as impellers of human action. However, there are views, especially from a scientific point of view, that question the validity of some of these – a claim that not all are impellers per se. The claim is that one or more of these are not basic impellers of human action, i.e. they are not a result of discovery, but rather derived inventions used by intelligent and resourceful human leaders to tame the human beast.

While that debate can be avoided here, it can be mentioned that there are valid reasons, discussed in chapter 6, that suggest that one can skip the attempt to find proof for the alternate hypotheses to the Purusharths model suggested above. In any case, an interesting outcome arises, if one acknowledges only two of the four as true impellers. This discussion becomes an important corollary obtained from the 'purusharths' theory/model. It brings out the root of the contrast between the 'material' and the 'spiritual' perspectives of life.

The two-impeller perspective: There are many who are convinced—and much of modern management education is based on this premise—that there are only two impellers 'Kama' and 'Artha' natural to humans. There is a conviction here that people will pursue only these two to their logical conclusion. It is believed in this perspective, that one ought to design, conduct and review life with the understanding that the two impellers are all there is to it… One can sum up this belief as, *"in the achievements of the objects/goods of 'kama' and 'artha' urges alone, exists happiness"* (the belief of the materialist).

In fact this system of thought also allows for people to indulge in some actions that are otherwise categorized under the Dharma urge. For example, one can consider work done for maintaining order and justice in society, as being an outcome of the desire to satisfy 'kama' and 'artha' urges; the sense of justice, is seen here to be a component of the 'burden' of 'social contract'—contracts which humans make with one another so that coexistence is possible. "I respect your space, you respect mine." "My freedom to swing my hand is limited by your right to not get struck and vice versa." "I get my 'kama' and 'artha' urges satisfied and you get yours satisfied - both to the optimum best possible and with justice to all humans."

In this perspective therefore, work towards sustaining rule-of-law is done in the spirit of give-and-take. The responsibilities in the rule-of-law would be 'duties' which people have to 'painfully' take up in order that they can earn a remuneration. With that remuneration, they can later on enjoy the fruits of their labor—in entertainment and other pleasurable things.

In this two impeller perspective, 'religions' would be seen as attempts made by some outstanding individuals towards 'encouraging' people into getting into 'disciplined' living. They could also be construed as efforts towards providing 'mental relief to oppressed individuals'. It is believed that the outstanding individuals get something out of it - that they are driven by their self-seeking needs related to self-actualization. The others who listen to these outstanding individuals and act accordingly, are also believed to benefit from it because they are, in turn, able to execute the pursuit of their Kama and Artha urges better through the disciplining.

This overall perspective of life can be called as the two-impeller perspective or the 'material' perspective of life.

The four-impeller perspective: The Purusharth model's four-impeller perspective, in contrast to the material perspective, offers the 'spiritual' perspective. It conveys that all four impellers are in fact equivalent in that they are all 'needs' of individuals. It suggests that individuals are engaged in a constant attempt to find 'completeness' through ALL of them. Just as the material nature of man's body can impel him to respond to certain urges, his divine nature is also supposed to impel him to respond to the urges of

Dharma and Moksha. In other words, this perspective conjectures man to contain a spiritual dimension in, addition to his material and social dimensions.

Those who vouch for this 'spiritual' perspective stake claim that they have learnt great secrets about human beings through a 'close observation' of subtler facts about human nature. Those who revel in the modern scientific method, can best understand these claims to insights, as an advancement over the modern scientific findings of the discipline of 'Transcendental Psychology'. This four-impeller perspective stakes claim to a deeper exploration of what Maslow described as 'Peak and plateau experience'—a deeper grasp of the metaphysical nature of man's behavior.

Seen from the reference frame of the 'material' perspective, the 'spiritual' perspective may appear as being a result of a deliberate move away from man's 'natural' urges to behave out of self-interest. . However, for practitioners who understand the spiritual perspective or alternatively have faith in it, the four-impeller model is a 'reality'—they say it is the true 'nature' of man.

Outcomes of using four impellers: The conviction in the four-impeller perspective, in turn, impacts the practical life of the believer. When a group, tribe, caste or an individual takes to this 'spiritual' four-impeller belief, they collectively infuse, observe and preserve traditions which reflect that belief. Such groups and individuals practice certain 'noble' traditions. Such change in behavior (ennobling traditions) reflects on the outcomes of their togetherness. Groups of people can take to a variety of positions on the four impellers and following are some positions of significance:

Group behavior based on the impeller models: An interesting distinction becomes evident when groups of people subscribe to one or the other of these theories. This serves to throw more light on the reason the wise men chose to recommend one of them.

Groups that are aware of two impellers only: The wise men have pointed out that when groups of people are restricted to a belief that the motivations of Kama & Artha alone exist, it adversely influences their excellence. Team goals are also set on the basis of the two impeller model. An individualistic perspective therefore, is sought to be collectively applied in society. Team work is indeed taken up, but the collective effort will ultimately be pervaded by self-seeking goals. In such societies, there does exist the scope for exhibiting behavior known as 'altruism' which is related to conscientious behavior. However, this is always taken up in full awareness of a conviction that human nature desires otherwise. The society definitely admires such altruism, but it is usually considered outside the norm, or unnatural.

Groups that 'know' the four-impeller model: Those who know the four-impeller model to be a true reflection of human nature, are also aware that the very knowledge of the nature of the four impellers produces many desirable qualities in individuals. These include greater productivity and better relationships. Being aware of the excellent qualities inspired within those who believe in the four impellers, these groups of people facilitate and patronize such collective learning. They teach this to the children. They ensure that this awareness is imparted to others though through the stories they recount. They select their leadership on this basis. Eventually such groups rise to execute the pursuit of their tasks better than others.

Groups acting out of faith in the wise: Awareness and understanding of the tenets of the four-impeller model is not easy for the average person. Many people are not able to benefit from the direct knowledge about it. However, the systems and traditions in society are designed in such a way that the benefits do still accrue to all members of a society. The general population still benefits through the practice of the traditions thus instituted. When the general population rigorously/religiously follow the traditions established by the wise (eg. of valor and nobility), they allow that 'hidden' wisdom to enrich their lives.

The Ramayana and Mahabharata are a celebration of this. As people listen to, share, and study the stories, the need for one to stand up for his Dharma is reinforced in them. All one needs to do in a society that is conversant with these stories is to say, "please do your Dharma," and the one who is being motivated is reminded of the call to Arjuna to let down his despondence, indulgence and melancholy and to take to righteous action. This instills in each member of the audience, the ability to raise their consciousness and apply themselves to their tasks with greater singlemindedness. Through this system, the wisdom about Dharma and Moksha cease to be matters that need to be imparted academically. They become realities that even illiterates pursue, as they go about their daily chores.

We can therefore conclude that the four purusharths model is a powerful tool for practical application in daily life—and Dharma is an integral part of it.

The universality of such traditions: It is really not necessary that civilizations and groups totally grasp the import of the four impellers. Just as altruism is integral to societies that profess allegiance to only two basic impellers, if one were to look at the traditions of bravery and nobility across the world, it would be evident that all four impellers are admired - albeit subtly. Consider any known war hero from across the world, any acknowledged work of altruism, any truly inspired performance, consider any of the admired heroes in the world of sports or politics... one would find that their attitude and bearing reflects the acknowledgment of the existence of motives even beyond the two primary ones.

It may not be always true that people choose a nobler path out of an understanding that there are four impellers... they may do it purely out of a gut feeling. People often feel deep within, that they can pay lower priority to the two basic impellers in favor of 'higher' aspirations. Often, people initially think they would like to do altruistic works as an extension of their commitment to the 'social contract'; having done this, they subsequently go on to experience a strange delight. This leads them to do more of it, just to get a kick out of it. In other words, a feeling of wellness can inspire people to behave in certain ways and follow certain traditions (that are otherwise recommended by the wise)—without mentally being aware of the existence of the four impellers.

People can go even as far as giving up their lives. Despite the fact that the four-impeller model is not popular knowledge across the world, bravery is indeed a global phenomenon. This happens because of strong traditions. Even if 'awareness' of the two additional impellers may be missing, traditions do help people practice those virtues of nobility. People, all over the world, do this.

In summary: One might well be truthful, honest and sincere in belief, in chasing the Kama and Artha impellers all through life, thinking it the be all and end all of existence; yet still, he may end up in utter discontent from the failure to address other deeper needs of his own. *"…And of what shall it profit a man if he gained the whole world but loses his soul…"* (Mark 8:36,). This passage from the bible reflects the same concept. If we liken the soul to the cause of the Dharma and Moksha urges, one can achieve wholeness to human life only through the pursuit of these.

The lack of this wholesomeness, we can see, is the problem with many individuals and it has reached epidemic proportions in modern life. We find many individuals who are focused, greedy and single-minded in the pursuit of Kama and Artha urges to the complete neglect of their sense of Dharma. What results is Adharma. It ends in misery for those that indulge in it and it adversely affects society – creating poverty, wretchedness and injury in others.

And he went on to say to them all, "Watch out and guard yourselves from every kind of greed; because your true life is not made up of the things you own, no matter how rich you may be." Jesus Christ: Luke 12:15 (Good News Translation)

To dissuade people from this tendency to get lost in the yen for Kama and Artha, the current leadership (political, economic, intellectual, spiritual and military) must inculcate a more holistic perspective. There is need for a major shift towards understanding and pursuing Dharma and Moksha in addition to the other two impellers. The leaders must move the general population, as also organizations and systems, towards the higher/nobler thought process. Those that are ignorant of these subtleties need to be enlightened, and those that are aware need to be promoted and facilitated.

4 DHARMA FROM FIRST PRINCIPLES: FOUR ASPECTS

"A progressive society chooses a Dharma which benefits most members of that society. Hence, Dharma has to change with time. While Dharma is an ancient concept, it must incorporate new principles to keep pace with changing times. The blind observation of any principle can only lead to failure, miseries and unhappiness."

— Awdhesh Singh, Myths are Real, Reality is a Myth

The Mahabharata offers us some clues as to what Dharma is. The term 'Dharma' is used in two different ways in this epic. When lord Krishna says that his role in this earth is to 'establish Dharma', the term 'Dharma' is being used as if to mean 'System' or 'order' in society—that is, Lord Krishna's role was to set up a 'system living the inspiration of righteousness'.

When Arjuna is told to 'do his Dharma', the term is being used more in the sense of Arjuna having a 'righteous duty' in a righteous system.

Then the question arises as to who defines what a person's (Arjuna's) duty is... the answer is that it is defined by someone who is 'Self-realized'.

We have not defined this term so far in the book, but for the moment let us presume that it is of the highest distinction in the spiritual world, where a person becomes the best he can be.

The next thing that is obvious is that duty is not the same for everyone in society. If it was Arjuna's duty to fight, it was his wife's duty to take care of the home. Besides, the defined set of duties in society definitely varies from time to time depending on the level of technology. For example, we did not have the pilots' duty about a century and a half ago because there were no airplanes at that time. Similarly, Dharma, in the sense of it being a duty roster, will also vary on geographical basis. For example, the tasks an inhabitant in the forest would have to complete will be different from the tasks for an individual in a desert. Dharma is thus task, time, place and system dependent.

All these considerations lead to unraveling four important dimensions, aspects or interdependencies of Dharma. They are as follows.

The First aspect of Dharma: The Supreme Self

There is an ethereal 'equality' at death. Another thing that nature has given to all humans in equal measure is laughter—regardless of disparity. Reasoning along these lines, outstanding philosophers, thinkers and saints have claimed that the 'substantive thing' in each one of us—the only thing in each of us that is of worth—is the same; and that we are all equal because of it.

Now, is it even correct to hazard that there is such a thing that can be described as 'the only thing of worth'—something of substance without which all in man is meaningless…? The following example will throw light.

Consider a billiards cue stick. Assume that the cue has abilities of imagination and memory. It can remember all the shots played and it can imagine itself to be anything.

Every time a shot is played on a billiards table, the cue-ball is struck by the tip of the cue. There is therefore at least one perspective, from which it will appear as if the cue is the author of each shot—just because it is only the cue that physically hits the cue-ball. Yet we know that it is the billiards player who is actually taking decisions and making the shots—we don't give credit to the cue for having attained some result in a game. The cue however, feels that 'it' is responsible for everything because it is unable to 'see' that there is someone else who is calling the shots...

We now shift the perspective a step backwards. How about the man who is using the cue? Is he the one who is truly pulling the shots? Is he, instead, also a cue – a medium through which something else is actually driving things? Between the cue-stick and the person, we see that the person is the one in whom the substance rests; similarly between the body-mind mechanism of the person, and a Supreme Power that is within the person, can it be said that the Supreme Power is the thing that must be given credit?

There is another way to see this... we may say "my forehead is as warm as the rest of my body." This implies that the forehead and the body are being considered as being separate from 'me' – the 'me' possesses them. Similarly, when someone says "the thought arose in my own mind," it implies that the mind too is being perceived as separate from 'me'.

What is this therefore, that is referred to as 'me'?

This is the puzzle which students of spirituality (those pursuing Gyan Yoga—the path of knowledge) are expected to unravel... The conclusion of the 'wise', is that the body is indeed a mere instrument; it is another thing of substance—Purusha—that animates the (inanimate) bodies, making the bodies alive.

Of this Purusha, it is said…

1)   It is beyond the senses. It is the source of peace and happiness. People, who realize the harmony and stand merged as it, emanate peace and happiness. Their personal merits improve drastically and excellence becomes their way of life.

2)   Persons who live in harmony with this force within themselves are able to know what the force within the rest of the people is doing. They are able to say exactly what reverberates/resonates with the hearts of individuals around them. Such peoples' goals, ambitions and delights become impersonal. They claim, 'I know me, so I know everyone', 'I know what "I" want and what I want is what everyone else truly wants'. In Christian terminology the 'I Am' knows what the 'I Am' in the other people wants. (Refer book 'Yogyathwa: Simple access to powerful leadership' for this concept)

The characteristics that accrue to such a person—who has discovered his true self—are known to be phenomenal. It is said that meritorious leaders radiate many if not most of these phenomenal characteristics. The discovery of the true self is known to lead to the flowering of the individual's highest potential, creativity and charisma. For them, all humans are equitable because they see themselves in everyone and find that the inequalities are insubstantial. In other words, such people are in no doubt that it is the 'One Spirit' who they truly are… that their bodies and minds are merely a covering or a shell—that, metaphorically speaking, they are the water in the ocean-wave and not the wave itself

One would ask, how is all this related to 'Dharma'? When a people achieve this distinction, i.e. when they know who they and others truly are, and when they entertain no doubt about it, they are said to be self-realized. The self-realized soul acts on behalf of 'everyone' and begins setting up systems and procedures in society that are good for all. In essence, the evolution from being a lesser mortal to being the Supreme Self happens in the following manner: I think and know that 'I am the body'; therefore, I think that I am limited and localized. Eventually, on discovery that I am impersonal, I lose the special attachment for the body and love my neighbor as myself. I discover the shared oneness with all others. 'I' become this 'new self' that knows itself to be 'unlimited'! The individual person thus surrenders to the 'Highest Self' or the 'Supreme Self' – and the 'Highest Ideal known to man' becomes manifest in him. Post this, the actions the person engages in, begin to reflect the qualities and aspirations of the 'Supreme Self'

In conclusion, since the 'Self Realized' speak on behalf of all, their words and works lead to the establishment of Dharma…

The first component of "Dharma" is therefore the will (desire) and concern of this 'Supreme Self'.

Is the 'Supreme Self' in operation today? Yes!

Is the will of the 'Supreme Self' being used today? Surely in spiritual and faith endowed institutions and individuals. But everyone has glimpses of the will of the 'Supreme Self' in its diluted substitutes listed here under:

1. The 'collective wisdom of humans'

2. The 'common human will'—as expressed in an 'ideal' democracy

3. The teaching, practice and traditions of wise ancestors—as expressed in the scriptures.

The Second aspect of Dharma: Rule of law

For a significant period in ancient India, the type of government that flourished was monarchy. In reality, it was not designed to be absolute dictatorship of one person—surely not in the Indian subcontinent. To understand this, let us consider the ceremonies that happened during the coronation of the king. One particular ritual in the ceremonies consisted of the Chief Priest of the kingdom chasing the king-designate around the throne with a staff in his hand—as if to beat him. The two of them would run three circles of the throne in this manner.

Why this ritual? Why was it a part of the coronation ceremonies?

The answer is that the king-designate was supposed to remember that the staff of 'Dharma' would always be chasing him when he sits on the throne. He is not to act arbitrarily; he must act according to what is ordained by 'Dharma'. This of course does not mean abdicating his responsibilities to whims of the Chief Priest. He must act according to Divine Will.

In other words, rule-of-Dharma, or its lesser cousin, rule-of-law – was paramount—not the whim of the king or the whim of anyone else. Note therefore that the Indian King was not a dictator. The king was to realize that he was merely playing a part in the rule-of-law and he had to behave accordingly. That is, he must derive his authority from the togetherness of all his citizens. 'Dharma' would be the sustainer of his kingdom instead, not individuals; not even the king himself. The king had to realize that power flowed 'through' his individuality and not 'from' his individuality…

Another curious question is related to why he was chased around the throne. He could have been merely told that he is not dictator and rule-of-law will prevail; it could have been groomed into him when he was in the process of learning… why make a visible spectacle of it?

The answer lies in the question… It was important to make a visible spectacle of it because the message was also for all others, just as it was for the King himself. Rule of law would prevail in the land; if it applied to the king, it applied to all power wielders in the kingdom… be it petty chiefs, principals, husbands, ministers, owners, mothers, caste leaders - it applied to anyone who was given designated powers in formalized institutions within that kingdom and in that society.

Similarly, when seen from the perspective of an executive in a present day company, it is important that he looks at his designation and role as a part of the processes that sustains the entire organization. Obedience by his juniors is not to him, it is to the system. He must facilitate; he must teach his juniors to respect the system and inspire them to play to its rules—rather than perceiving it as if he is driving it—even if he were the owner.

Note that when shifting from the 'Individuals-are-drivers' perspective to a 'Individuals-are-participants-in-rule-of-law' perspective, the tasks that individuals will be expected to take on in an organization remain the same. However, while 'Individuals-are-drivers' is an 'attached' point of view, the 'Individuals-are-participants-in-rule-of-law' leads to detachment from one's role; in this there is a powerful shift towards excellence. This in turn helps in better shouldering of the responsibilities.

Therefore, the second principle in 'Dharma' pertains to the establishment of the "the rule-of-law—as desired by the 'Supreme Self'…"

The Third aspect of Dharma: Sublimation of the Sense of Duty through Higher Consciousness

Consider a system that is up and running, consonant with what has been considered so far. The 'Supreme Self' has designed the system and each person has a role in it. When each one plays his part, the system is sustained, and it may be said that all those playing a part in the system are upholding it. Also, when the system is running as designated by the Supreme Self, the interests of 'All Humans' are automatically protected. For it is the basic premise of the 'Supreme Self', that the 'Universal Self'—cutting across 'all' categories of Humans—is everybody's self.

The wise therefore encourage people to do their 'duties' in 'Dharma'—after all it is going to be the system, and the rule-of-law, that will deliver its goods to all humans; or as Adi Sankara says "Dharma is the greatest benefactor" (Prashnottara Ratnamalika).

In addition to calling for duties to be done in 'Dharma', the wise also tell their wards to do their duty without expectations, keeping only welfare and the aspirations of the 'Supreme Self' in their minds. This leads to an important consequence…

The general connotation we have of duty, is that it is something we feel 'compelled' to do, and that it is what 'someone else' desires. We may be doing the job that the manager of a factory has delegated to us; we do that duty/job as something that needs to be done in the interests of receiving something in return; I get my remuneration at the end of the month, and from that salary, I can buy things to satisfy my needs… This is the classical perspective from the two impeller theory.

Now consider those things you do which you believe needs to be done because you want that thing done. When done, it fulfills something which is your deepest desire… You are convinced it must happen; you personally want it to happen. So if you are doing something leading to what you desire, is there a duty in it?

Let us understand this using a metaphoric reference. If it is a certain teacher's desire that students must learn their manners and the teacher is also teaching them manners, then the teacher is doing his 'own' thing, where is the question of the duty the teacher is executing?

Take another example: when the founder of a school started it, he was concerned with the education of the students in that region - that was the main reason why he started the school. When a teacher belonging to the school teaches there, he can either teach in order to 1) do his duty (and legitimately take his salary at the end of the month). Alternatively, 2) by having a desire that the students in this area need to be taught, he could be doing his 'own' thing while teaching… In the first case, the Owner is looking at the welfare of the people and the teacher is basically motivated by his salary. In the second case, the teacher also has the same motivates as the owner. Therefore, in the latter case, the teacher's will and the will of the founder of the organization merge.

Is the teacher doing his duty in the second case? Or is he ensuring realization of his deepest desires…with the salary coming by itself in the end of the month, as part of the system?

This is what is amazing about 'Dharma'. When one does their part selflessly in a 'Dharma', their will matches with the will of the "Supreme Self" which designed the society/dharma in the first place. Here comes the best part… If the "Supreme Self" is doing its role in the 'system'- which of course it has designed according to its own wishes - then is it doing a 'duty'?

The answer is no!!

When a person is doing his work in a dharmic system and does not feel he is doing a duty he achieves convergence with the 'Supreme Self'. He is said to have taken to yoga and the characteristics of the Supreme Self manifests in him… Peace, contentment, excellence, prosperity, charisma. Everyone knows that these people are enjoying their work…

We thereby come to one of the important statements from ancient Indian wisdom…

"For one that has attained Supreme Self, there is no duty!" (Bhagwad Gita)

Inducements do not motivate such a person. It is rather the opportunity, to act his part in the righteous system. The environment that is created around a person who enjoys his work, who has found convergence with the Supreme Self, is said to be Dharmic. He is tuned to excellence and has an induction effect - inspiring excellence in the people around him.

This is what a Christian desires for when he prays "Thy will be done" … Doing the Father's Will, he becomes one with The Father and With Jesus Christ.

A leader will therefore help his fellowmen gain a Dharmic attitude. In so doing he will be attempting to shift people from the frame of 'self-indulgence' to that of 'selflessness'. He will be impelling them towards the upkeep of Dharma for he knows that an environment of excellence is nurtured amongst people who participate in a system bearing an attitude that their work is not 'duty'; that their work is what they themselves will.

That is the third aspect of dharma… in Dharma, 'duty' is about raising work to the level of 'selflessness' by which there will be 'no duty'. The person who is practicing Dharma, is elevated in consciousness into the sphere of the Supreme Self!

The Fourth Component: Era specificity

As time flows, technological advances happen; different periods in history, therefore, demand different requirements from people. There are also geographical variations on the globe and the needs of people in the various regions will be different. Different kinds of administrative systems can be chosen (e.g. democracy/communist) in different nation states. Such variation mandates that there cannot be one fixed pattern of duties or a rigidly defined "Dharma".

Given the contextual nature of existence, there is a need from time to time, for those who are tuned to the 'Supreme Self', to either fine tune pre-existing systems, or re-design them completely so that it resonates with that particular age and location.

In the twenty-first, century a soldier cannot be told that his dharma is to fight with the sword and the bow and arrow; today the times have changed and technology has brought in smart weapons completely changing terms of battle engagement. Similarly, considering geography, the ceremonies that people perform on the banks of the Ganges cannot be performed in the banks of the water bodies of Alaska or Siberia; someone who tries that at minus 40 degrees centigrade could possibly freeze to death!

Another example is about the role of the woman. Today when the world leaders have declared that the role of 'bread-earner' is ideally shared by the lady of the house, it cannot be told to a girl child that her Dharma is also to attend to all the needs of her husband and children single handedly. One cannot train a man to revel manhood and also ask his wife to share bread-winning, while leaving her to take care of all of the house work and be at the service of everyone at home. Wisdom needs to step in and re-tune or re-wire the system.

Though the roles of the sexes are a complex matrix varying from culture to culture, caste to caste and civilization to civilization, the fact that women are expected to be 'equal' to man according to Human Rights (an integral part of what is the accepted norm in this time and age), must lead to a natural change in roles... The Supreme Self would want that there is proper balance. This of course includes concerns not only regarding human rights, but also regarding families, nurturing of excellence in children and care for the elderly. Every social group needs to arrive at its own balance that is fair, equitable and comprehensive.

With change in time, with change in setting, if these systems are not tuned for the given context, they cease to be 'Dharmic' in the true sense of the word. Therefore the fourth component of Dharma is that it must be attuned to the times...

All systems should be checked to answer positively to the question,

'Is it Dharmic?' Justice must be done to all humans. A nation must ask itself whether the definition of 'Dharma', as expressed in its systems, is truly up-to-date, represents collective wisdom, and rule of law.

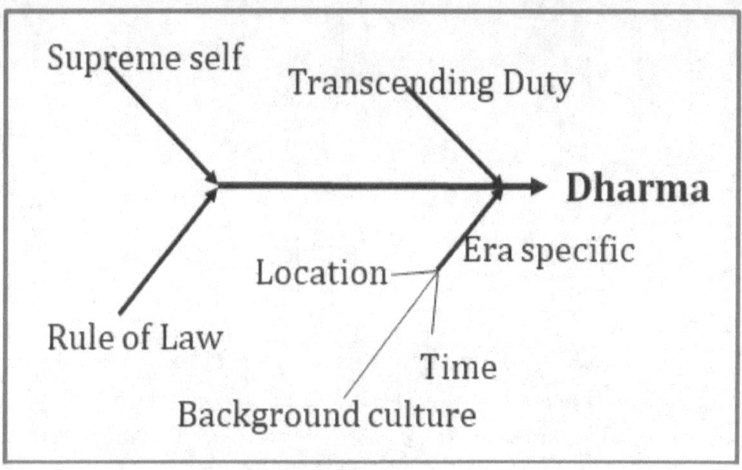

Conclusion: The diagram above summarizes for us the important aspects of the principle of Dharma dealt with in this chapter.

1. It is essentially driven by the "Supreme Self"—the best "Self" known to man.
2. It involves setting up a system (socio, political, economic, military etc.) that thrives in giving justice to every individual in society.
3. Even in a state of ignorance, individuals can participate in the system from a sense of duty, raising their consciousness towards the Supreme Self. Their Will merges with the Will of the "Supreme Self", which has designed the Dharmic system in the first place.
4. This Dharmic system is fine tuned to meet the requirements of the time, place and culture in which it is being applied.

5 DHARMA AND THE LEADER

They are not following dharma who resort to violence to achieve their purpose. But those who lead others through nonviolent means, knowing right and wrong, may be called guardians of the dharma. Those who really seek the path to Enlightenment dictate terms to their mind. Then they proceed with strong determination.

----Gautama Buddha

With awareness that oneness with the Supreme Self leads one to excellence, and understanding that excellence can transform an organization, the leader takes up activities that raises his consciousness towards the Supreme Self and facilitates others also towards the same.

A leader is self-assured that in Dharma there is a 'righteous system'—appropriate for the present moment and in the best interest of everybody. The leader is aware that when people do selfless work in Dharma, it helps them seek and attain the highest that humans can aspire. The leader is confident that nothing in the world can give the team as much joy as connecting with the Supreme Self.

Having seen that Dharma can do immense good to society and organizations, leaders promote it when they take up any position of authority. They facilitate Dharma and Excellence at all interfaces. They do their best to move the system at their disposal towards Dharma.

What are the areas that leaders focus on for execution, in order to uphold Dharma in and throughout their organization?

1) *The leader helps the organization set up Dharmic goals:* It is important that an organization must fit into the scheme of the overall system, which in turn is designed for the welfare of all of humanity (Dharmic). This will mean that the goals set by this team must also be in tune with an overall Dharmic ethos. Therefore, during the formation of the team, there is a need for proper aligning of interests of the stake holders in a manner that the collective befits Dharma. The leader prods the organization to make choices and take decisions that make it a partner to and participant in Dharma.

2) *The leader helps set up an organizational structure conducive to Dharma:* Having defined the overall role of an organization in Dharma, the next task would be the actual design and construction of the organization. This requires managerial inputs that leaders bring to the table by themselves, or with the help of experts. The core intent of the leaders however, is to ensure that the structure established is indeed conducive to the thriving of the 'Supreme Self' in the team members. It includes ensuring that the relationships and interactions that are defined between individuals, (at all levels and across all functions in an organization) are conducive to bringing out the best from the members of the team/organization.

3) *The leader helps the organization take Dharmic decisions as it goes along:* Having formalized the role and design of the organization, the leaders' next task is that of running it. The

primary role of a leader in running an organization is in making decisions on its behalf. These decisions must be made in accordance with the wishes of the 'Supreme Self'. That is, when the organization navigates through its field of action, a leader keeps it anchored along the path of Dharmic Excellence and his decisions reveal this aspect.

4) *The leader stimulates fellow workers to raise their levels to inspiration:* This definitely is the most visible distinguishing feature of a leader. Leaders inspire; and as they say in military parlance—even for the ultimate sacrifice. This feature of leadership cannot be understood in any other way than through acknowledging the spiritual nature of man. Something about the leader - what he says and does, his bearing, his thoughts - all have this inherent ability to raise people above their 'individual-personal-interests' and make them take up larger causes. This aspect cannot be imitated—it is at the level of experience and it manifests as 'authority' in a leader. Having given up individual interests, the followers emerge happy from their work feeling…'we did it!'. As Lord Krishna tells Arjuna at the battle field in the Bhagwad Gita, "Slain in battle, you will attain to heaven, victorious you will enjoy the earth".

Summarizing the above four tasks of a leader in Dharma we can say that true leader becomes a guardian of Dharmic interests…

A leader ensures that the cause for which the collective works, lies within the ambit of Dharma. Right from the conception to its construction and through its running, the leader checks every aspect of the organization against the litmus test of whether what is happening is in accordance with Dharma. Leaders must therefore allow the spirit of Dharma to flow in their veins; it must grow up to be a part of their personality and culture. They must always remember that enduring organizations are built on Dharma alone and must desist from losing focus on this at any stage.

Raising Dharma to its rightful highest place

The recommended primacy of Dharma is evident from the list above, which 'explains' it through the role of a leader in any togetherness. This primacy can also be seen in a different way by referring to the 'feel' for the 'action' a leader must take up.

It is said that when there is a conflict in society, in order to resolve it, the following steps must be taken in sequence (ascending order) until the conflict is resolved:

Level I. Common Practice: If there is a conflict, first refer to "Common Practice" and try to resolve it. If it does not get resolved then go to the next higher parameter

Level II. Traditions: Find what traditions have to say and try resolving the conflict. If it is still unresolved, go to the next level

Level III.   Books of Law: Refer to "Books of Law" to determine what is right. If law too, is not able to resolve it, then go to the highest level.

Level IV.   Dharma: The highest reference to resolve issues is "Dharma", where one refers to the will of the Supreme Self.

Clearly, this list places "Dharma" at the highest position. This is because dharma, as we have already seen, relates intimately to the essential nature of man—to the "Supreme Self" - and it relates to everybody equitably. This essential 'divine' nature of man impels the proper design of the laws made to govern humans. Therefore, Dharma is even more than just rule-of-law; it signifies both - that which is codified in law and that which is not. It operates at a level of "Feeling" and therefore addresses every possible human relationship and interaction. Dharma instructs on how one must interact with the spouse, children, parents, friends, workmen, seniors, colleagues... how one must treat animals and plants... how one must take care of his body, how one must eat his food, how he must spend his time... It is about how a mother takes care of her child. It is about how a doctor takes care of his patient, about how a warrior must go to battle... It even says how one must interact with his Guru, with the priests in one's religion—which ever religion. It instructs how one must approach one's work, life, relationships, the deities one worships, possessions, aspirations... everything. It is all about spirituality. It is about everything a human being can do and it involves checking whether it is being done in the interests of the Supreme Self. It is based on a universality that transcends all kinds of groups. Dharma is the religion of living... Tej Guru Sirshree says "Dharma is your very nature, just as the nature of water is to flow". Dharma is the nature of the Supreme Self.

The primary role of the Leader with respect to Dharma

Most men are lost in the pursuit of only Kama and Artha in life. All that matters to them is what they get in terms of satisfying their bodies' urges or in terms of the status they achieve in life and/or the material possessions they accumulate. People who have such an approach are said to be lost in ignorance. This ignorant pursuit is known to create great misery for the people who see themselves in a rat-race.

Leaders infuse the sense of Dharma in their followers; they transform their limiting pursuit of only Kama and Artha into an exalted process that is at the same time liberating and joyous; thus opening for their followers, a gate to Nirvana.

In other words, the leader instills detachment in the followers so that their pursuit of satisfying Kama and Artha urges gets transformed into a delightful pursuit; and Nirvana takes center stage instead.

This is the basic definition of a leader... This is his basic role

Therefore, bosses, people who are given authority in any system or organization, are truly leaders if and only if their disposition, their decisions and their actions inspire juniors, peers and seniors alike, to transition to higher levels of consciousness. Excellence is but natural in such organizations and success and prosperity follows.

In Summary

Leaders must facilitate others' pursuit of the 'highest ideal' and must pursue it themselves. They must participate in establishing and sustaining the rule of law and ensure that the law is updated according to the times. They must facilitate everyone to participate in the best of their ability. By infusing a sense of dharma into the mundane life of followers lost in the pursuit of objects that satisfy Kama and Artha urges, the leader inspires them to contentment and excellence and facilitates for them the gate to nirvana.

6 SCIENTIFIC VALIDATION OF METAPHYSICAL CONCEPTS

The Dharma is a very, very special and precious thing. The more you practice it, the more you will realize this.

----Tenzin Palmo

Up to this point in the book, we have dealt with several 'Theories' or 'Models' that attempt to describe a phenomenon in the metaphysical world, a phenomenon called Dharma. These are likely to be familiar and unfamiliar at the same time; while most Indians can relate to the subject under discussion, all readers may not necessarily be familiar with the nitty-gritty of the models. It is possible that the models have been alien to the cultural setting of the reader. Therefore, it will take some time and effort to get accustomed to. In order to help readers grasp the utility of the models better, it is important to summarize by taking a bird's eye view of some of them that we have reckoned. This exercise helps address the question of validity or invalidity of the model overall. With this purpose in mind let us again take a look at the models we have considered in the preceding sections. Briefly, the following are the models:

The four-impeller model of motivation

This is a model that we considered in which four impellers are recognized; Dharma, Artha, Kama and Moksha. This theory raises Dharma and Moksha, which were considered as optional choices in earlier theories, to equivalence with Artha and Kama in that all four are needs or drivers. In fact, Dharma and Moksha are considered the primary drivers in human nature for attainment of true bliss—they are said to be unavoidable and powerful components governing human behavior. One can demonstrate true leadership only if they understand and acknowledge this higher nature of man….

The Concept of the Supreme Self:

This model has to do with the 'self' that each person relates to. That which the wise term as the highest possible of these 'selves' is called as the Supreme Self. The connotation to 'highest' being akin to what we observe in the act of a jeweler who when he finds a rare gem, proceeds to sell everything else he owns to acquire that rare one. The model says that people can act from this state even without knowing that they are in such state. Having discovered the Supreme Self, when an individual merges in it and identifies himself with that state, to the exclusion of all other states—he becomes wise. Such a person is said to be self-realized. He is has attained Nirvana. This Supreme Self is also studied under transcendental studies. The other states are known to be ignorant states and rising above these and entering to selflessness, one attains the Supreme Self.

The model of the Universal Brahman

We had a fleeting reference to the term "Purusha" earlier in the book. This is a component in the model of the Universal Brahman (entire Universe). The other component is Prakriti. Every human creature is a combination of the two principles. When the human creature identifies itself with an illusionary 'individual' who gets created in the meeting point of the two principles of Purusha and Prakriti, it is said to be in ignorance. The illusion clears when the creature understands that it is the impersonal Purusha itself. Basis this realization, the highest potential of the person is unleashed... Yoga helps the person shift from the lower to the higher spheres. It is said that Self Realization is nothing but the Purusha identifying itself in a given creature. Therefore, the Purusha in each individual is nothing but the Universal Supreme Self.

Dharma and its four components:

We have also sought to understand Dharma through its four components. Though it is not an established model in as far as the scriptures are concerned, this elaboration of the idea is best discerned in this manner. It has these four aspects namely the Supreme Self, a system operating on Rule-of-law, Transcending Duty and Era specific nature. The fish bone diagram in the previous chapter puts these aspects in perspective. Each of the aspects can be studied for its relation with the other three; and all four together en-frame the totality of the Dharma concept.

Important conclusions from the models:

The Supreme Self Theory and the Theory of the Universal Brahman models suggest that the person who has come out of ignorance achieves excellence. They suggest that when people are out of ignorance they become worthy of leadership as many of their talents bloom to the full. Of the two theories, the Supreme Self Theory makes a distinction between people who are liberated from bondage and those who are not; the Theory of the Universal Brahman, additionally hints at a process by which a person can shift from ignorance to excellence. According to this latter model, ignorance can be dispelled when a person 'Realizes' his true nature. Therefore, this model shows us that self-perception plays an important role in setting the destiny of an individual.

The Theory of the Universal Brahman further suggests that the process by which a person may realize 'His true nature' are twofold. One is the method of reason and thought, called as the path of knowledge. The other is called as the path of yoga; yoga loosely meaning 'exercises', which an ignorant person can take up, which by themselves, will eventually land him into 'wisdom' — even if just temporarily.

Finally, the totality of the models suggests that taking to yoga and the pursuit of Dharma are the key principles for excellence in life. While the process of taking to yoga is capable of lifting a person to touch his highest potentials, the pursuit of Dharma is capable of lifting a group/team of people to their highest potential in conjunction with individual excellence. The wise men of yore have insisted that lives lived without either taking to yoga or Dharma are lived in vain…

Scientific credibility of these theories/models

Clearly, the above four models consist of various terms that are unfamiliar to the scientific world – for instance Supreme Self, Dharma and Kama. There could be equivalents and close substitutes for these terms in western literature, but these definitions are unique to the line of thinking that has been normal in the Indian Subcontinent.

One can definitely wonder whether all these words are mere contraptions or whether they are observables. If they are observables, how does one locate them and therefore obtain proof for the elaborate nature of these proposed theories? This is no mean task. Sages have spent lifetimes over it. Yet others say that it is close at hand and all it takes is a 'eureka' moment. The debate seems to go in favor of the latter argument because if Dharma has been designed in a manner that it can be practiced by lay persons in society, there must be something to it that is within an average man's grasp.

In the interest of using rational analysis, it is important at this stage to draw a parallel with an important theory in Physics so that the rational thinker may be facilitated to give the above models more than a second thought…

Schrodinger was a research student in the 1930's, when he went to his guide and said that he had a gut feeling that if he mathematically represented matter particles as waves subjected to some kind of equations, there was a likelihood of coming up with a mathematical explanation to their basic behavior.

If one is aware, it was about that time (early 1930's) when physicists had come up with observations that matter particles behaved as if they were waves. Shrodinger's guide probably felt that it was a little over the top, but none the less, he encouraged him to pursue it further. What finally resulted was the Schrodinger Wave Equation; it turned out to be a mathematical marvel. Schrodinger proposed a set of 'rules' as to how this wave must be mathematically treated in terms of 'differential equations' (people not too keen on mathematics need not bother much about these). Some parts in the rules corresponded to energy, others to time and still others to space and so on. When the mathematical equations he so developed as problems were 'solved', they gave out results and figures that easily correlated with observations in nature.

To date no one knows why those rules work; why a certain energy term must be constructed in a particular way or why a certain constant must be used and not another… but it works! Though the 'wave' is central to this theory, no physicist in the world knows its composition. A probability distribution pattern can be calculated from the mathematical expression that represents the wave. This distribution gives a probabilistic idea of where the particle could be found; but they will not be able to say what the wave contains. In the case of light waves, we can say that it consists of electric and magnetic fields, but in quantum mechanical waves – no one knows. Yet the wave approach of Quantum Mechanics is an accepted theory in science today.

The reason for its acceptance is that it has successfully explained large volumes of observed data; that is, the theory's application is remarkably accurate. No scientist has been able to truly call to question this theory; all they can do now is wonder what this wave could possibly be, but admit – grudgingly - that there must be truth in it. The bottom line is that they still do not know what is 'matter wave' and though that be the case, it remains firmly at the heart of the theory they have come to accept.

The point being made here is that though the four models summarized here above do not subject themselves to mathematical analysis, and though they use seeming non-observables like 'Supreme Self', they do lead to reasonable applications that can be truly observed. It is true that a yogic attitude in a leader definitely inspires followers—and that would, in turn, make us wonder whether this elaborate theory and model of the Universal Brahman may have some truth in it after all… Nations, kingdoms, kings - people in general – who have taken to Dharma, truly have seen excellence, peace and prosperity… The application works… Good examples of this are the Maratha king Shivaji who was inspired by his teachers, and Harihara and Bukka who founded the Vijayanagara empire.

Having said this, there is one additional consolation—that many of the postulates made here, including that of the 'Supreme Self', are in fact observables! They are not observables in the same sense as the material observables, but in some other way—as claimed by many eminent men.

The argument is that even though the postulates cannot be proved, the theory finally does give out applications that can be tested; this should be enough to satisfy the student that the models hold weight. More importantly, if the reader/student searched smartly - in the right places - even the postulates will be obvious.

The reader/researcher must therefore inquire into the internal consistency of the models proposed here and pursue their application. At the outset, one needs to go by 'faith' that there may be truth in the models; that much is required in any learning process. But beyond that work must be done to pursue the application and observe the effect of the models. One can also pursue disciplines proposed by illustrious teachers (beware of ending up before half-baked Gurus. Check Appendix E:Who is wise?); personally pursuing the application and observing the truths by oneself is critical in metaphysical studies.

7 EVERYBODY PARTICIPATES: SOCIETY'S FOUNDATION PRINCIPLE IS 'GIVING'

The person who understands Dharma will have the opposite reaction to a "hard" job. That person will be eager to get started, no matter what kind of work is in front of her, because she understands that she's doing God's work. And when you're working for God, nothing is too hard.

----Russell Simmons

'This is our time' - this statement is true at all times; and is always made in the present. Each generation of humans has the right to choose how it lives. Looking backward there have been generations that exercised the choice and used the best of principles to live their lives. Other people at other times just let it drift; either not valuing high principles, or using those principles in a half-baked manner. In some generations, people misused these principles to play mischief and for personal benefit. The generations that failed to apply the best principles eventually bore the brunt of evil forces; negatively impacting their societies and their lives.

However, the very same principles have often been used to establish successful kingdoms (kingdoms are truly successful only when, as a collective, all the people of the nation are content).

The choice therefore is in the hands of the present generation - either make a mark in History as a generation that used the highest of principles to live exalted lives, or to waste it all. The principles are real; it is for the leader of the present generation to use them to elevate himself, his family, his organization, his nation and the world...

Even if an individual is bothered mainly about running a small organization (a nuclear family even), understanding of these eternal principles gives him excellent directions to choose, in his quest for successfully shouldering his responsibilities.

It is indeed instructive & critical, for people as a collective or as individuals, to look carefully and pay attention to the ways of the wise; to study & learn from how they thought and how they acted...

One thing common to all societies that prospered based on following high principles, is that in all of them, positive actions began with the discovery that living in the inspired way of the 'Supreme Self' was far superior to living the limited lives of ego bearing individuals. Once leaders crossed this landmark or tipping point in the journey of inner discovery, it becomes second nature for them to coax, advise, inspire and facilitate their fellow beings (and the institutions they have influence over), to move in the same direction. This has indeed been the story of heroism in all of history. Whether it has been struggles for freedom, struggles to preserve freedom, attempts to uphold justice, initiatives to transform nations, outstanding work of all kinds... the leadership in all of this invariably has crossed the tipping point and into various manifestations of the same idea—exalted and selfless living.

Self-Realization – and emanating from it – the Highest-Self-Expression, therefore becomes most important for the Leader. This represents the realization or manifestation of the power of the Supreme Self. Understanding its virtues and gifts, the leader revels in it and brings it forth for others to benefit from. Dharma remains the foremost way in which this was facilitated in society.

Dharma: Putting God in between: A sizeable portion of the wisdom contained in the ancient Indian scriptures, is presented for common man's understanding through the narration of legends, incidents and stories. Here is a narration that throws light on how Dharma works...

Lord Krishna (God-on-earth) and Arjuna (friend and warrior prince) were resting in a forest. Mayasura (probably a deified version of a variety of indigenous persons) approached them at that time and expressed gratitude to Arjuna for having saved his life earlier. He requested Arjuna to ask for something in return.

Arjuna would have none of it; according to his 'dharma' (he had the duties of the warrior), it was his duty to help those in distress and those who sought his help. Since he had merely done his duty, he could not take anything in return as compensation.

At the same time, it was Mayasura's duty to give something in return as a mark of gratitude; but Arjuna was refusing to take anything in return. Both were in a fix.

To resolve the problem, Arjuna suggested that Mayasura may do something that lord Krishna asked of him. The ball landed in Lord Krishna's court. Now Arjuna and his family, the Pandavas, did not have a proper place to stay, and Lord Krishna suggested to Mayasura,"why not build a house for them?" Mayayasura happily built for them a magnificent palace that was without rival-Indraprasta...

What does this narration convey?

The clue to it lies in the fact that Lord Krishna is acknowledged in the Indian pantheon of gods and goddesses to have realized his "Supreme Self"—he is known to be in constant touch with the true inner self. This gives him one of his numerous names: 'Stithpragya' (Stith – established; pragya – consciousness) it loosely translates to someone who is stabilized in the understanding that he is eternal spirit and the body is the covering. As such, he represented God on earth—always doing the Will of God; or better still – he harbored no individual will... So the entire take and give was being centered on Him—the Supreme Self; the lesson conveyed is that 'God' must be placed in the middle...

Both of them, Mayasura and Arjuna, by following their Dharma, are in fact working for the Supreme Self and it is the 'Supreme Self' that is giving to them in return—Dharma gave protection for Mayasura and Lord Krishna gave Arjuna a place to stay. In the process, both are taken care of. The focus is on giving—all people give to God and God gives them what they need.

That is why, in the societies developed around the idea of the Supreme Self, the concept of Dharma is used... People are advised to 'do their Dharma' or to 'Uphold Dharma'—this is the doing part. On the delivery end, we see that "Dharma is the greatest benefactor" (Adi Sankara); meaning that it is not people who give but rather it is the system that delivers—Dharma gives.

Therefore, at the heart of the matter, individualism is sacrificed and God is placed in the center; this is one of the basic precepts of 'Dharma' as seen earlier. It is the practical spiritual representation of this idea of 'Dharma'—encouraging people to do their work for the sake of God, trusting that God will take care of them in return.

Some people can be uncomfortable with the reference to divinity in the story narrated. However, that should not matter. Even if we dilute the object of our adoration 'God' and 'Supreme Self' to something more palatable to the agnostic and the atheist, like 'Common Human will', 'Humanity', 'social good', 'togetherness', 'selflessness', 'impersonal' and such other terms, it roughly points in the same direction. Therefore, instead of saying, "Do your

Dharma keeping God above everything," the agnostics and the atheists can be told, "do your duty keeping 'Humanity' above everything".

The moral of the story that we just considered is that people must look for their contentment in life by focusing on the 'impersonal' rather than looking for it in 'personal aggrandizement'. Through this alone can a righteous system, that does maximum good to everyone, be established—Dharma. Through being impersonal, the graces can be enjoyed by both the upholder of Dharma and by society itself. The leaders in society must therefore know that the right way to motivate their people is to encourage them to work for others. It is best for society and for the people who are being advised to work thus.

Pursuit of Dharma is about living a life of passion: The term Dharma is powerful because it makes it unnecessary for everyone in society to go to schools of spiritual learning; instead, even as the lay people do their normal day-to-day chores, they can develop an attitude of peace, focus, excellence in work and contentment. The greatest wealth, which the civilization knows of, is indeed available to everyone in society. Getting everyone to practice Dharma makes it possible. Dharma is capable of involving everyone in society in a human chain that works at making each other's life prosperous, sublime and blissful.

It is instructive to contrast this with the opposite perspective. In the alternate perspective, individuals, their needs and their rights become the centerpiece. Everyone is facilitated to live in the 'I need' mode. Each one is thinking of themselves and is in this race to capture for themselves as much as possible, from what they are told are 'scarce resources'. Studies have shown it leads to a lesser life with limited excellence, minimal peace, lesser contentment, less fruitful relationships, and people with untapped potential - forever living in anticipation of Joy.

An interesting depiction of this contrast is as follows: a group of people are sitting around a huge vessel of porridge with spoons having long handles but fused to their hands. The spoon handles are so long that the people cannot put the porridge into their mouths. In the self-seeking team, there are a lot of frustrated people unable to eat and in contrast, in the 'serve-others' team they are feeding each other and are enjoying the porridge.

8 THE CONSTITUTION DEFINES SYSTEMIC DHARMA FOR MODERN INDIA

Those who see worldly life as an obstacle to Dharma see no Dharma in everyday actions. They have not yet discovered that there are no everyday actions outside of Dharma.

----Dogen

If lord Rama were to be walking the earth today, what would Dharma be? What is the system he would have been obliged, duty-bound and dispassionately resolved to follow?

We know that though he was the crown prince, he went on exile. Though he never doubted the fidelity of his wife, he had to live separated from her and from his children. These decisions he took were on the basis of the Dharma of those times. Monarchy was in vogue and there were well established rules and principles for the functioning of monarchies. There were the injunctions to office bearers at the various levels about how to act and how not to act. These injunctions were built into the traditions that were in existence at that time and Lord Rama stood by those injunctions and traditions.

In that time and age, being the eldest son, Lord Rama was obliged to be King. That was in accordance with Dharma. No one else could be called to shoulder that responsibility before him; it was the role of the eldest son first. Whether he liked it or not, the burden of Kingship was upon him. Excellence in Dharma demanded that he sacrifice his family life and live separated from his wife and children.

Today, in the twenty first century, there is no monarchy in Ayodhya anymore. Ayodhya is part of India, and India has been constituted into a democracy. Today a Prime Minister leads the nation and the President is the nominated head of state; if Lord Rama were to shoulder either of the two roles, and if he was confronted with a situation where he had to choose between family and political suzerainty, would he be obliged to give up his family? Rather, would today's Dharma ask him to respect his vows as a husband and resign from the leadership post instead?

In the ancient Indian monarchy, besides the king, all other officials down the line had a Dharmic role to play. In today's society likewise, what is such role each stakeholder of today's society would have to play? What is the Dharma that an individual—in pursuit of enlightenment—would need to uphold?

In a very broad sense, Dharma is defined as the traditions and practices of honored ancestors. Does that mean that Indians must follow the traditions of wise ancestors who have lived thousands of years ago?

Not precisely so; we have already seen, that a change in era would necessitate a re-defining of Dharma. The lofty thinking of the ancients should inspire today's Dharma alright, but at the same time, it must be practically suited for the times. What then, is it that defines it for us?

Search for a Self-Realized soul:

If the system that we choose should have the seal of authority of the Supreme Self then we need to look out for self-realized souls and to ask them as to what would be good for us. However, it cannot be just any self-realized soul - the chosen one must have a deep understanding of how the present economic, democratic and scientific orders work.

In ancient India, though many individuals were recognized as self-realized souls, it was upon the scholar-king Manu to set up the basic constitution of Dharma. Do we have such a scholar amidst us - a self-realized soul who also understands the innards of polity?

A person close to this definition that we have had in modern times is Mahatma Gandhi. In some circles, he is considered a saint. He also took part in political affairs with awareness of modern systems. Being a barrister, he understood the rule of law as it existed in the modern context. As a spiritual leader he was able to raise the consciousness of a generation of people and inspire them for the kind of political activity that reflected the highest of values. MK Gandhi never staked a claim to perfection in self-realization, while surely several contemporaries have been acknowledged to have attained the highest: Ramana Maharishi and Nisargadatta Maharaj are two examples. Similarly, people have marveled at many outstanding political leaders and intellectuals, but an effective combination is hard to find. Spiritual lights of this day can surely guide when a specific question is put across to them. They would do outstandingly well in an 'enlightened Anarchy' that Gandhi Propounded. However, setting up a temporal power structure needs awareness of modern systems. It is not easy for someone not so well informed about modern systems, even if self-realized, to come up with a constitution of a practical overall system that can deliver the goods for a nation. Therefore, effectively, Gandhiji was the best available and only opportunity for the nation—a politically informed and wise soul. It is another matter that Gandhiji's constructive suggestions for free India could not be implemented in full measure due his untimely martyrdom.

How then, does one resolve the issue of a suitable Dharma for the times as being willed and designed by the Supreme Self?

What is the substitute for the Self Realized soul?

The scientific world has flourished for around six centuries now. Let us call this the Scientific Civilization. The scientific method, which is at the core of the Scientific Civilization, is indeed based on the pursuit of truth. The scientific method has evolved into a system that gathers knowledge, preserves it, builds on it and effectively transfers it to the next generation. The economic order, which the 'free world' has accepted, does have its handicaps, but it has performed better than any of the other systems that were tested in the present world. Democracy has also emerged as the best amongst the systems of government. People do say Democracy is bad, but it is the best among others that are even worse. As democracy evolved, it has incorporated within itself many working principles. These include checks and balances, division of powers, separation of religion and state, protection of minorities, affirmative action, preservation of Human rights, and so on. Many scholars and political leaders have elaborated upon these. Effectively, over the centuries, successful peoples and nations seem to have given us democracy, capitalism, the scientific method and several such ideals as the bouquet of solutions that are best pursued for the welfare of humanity.

Is this therefore the best?

Among the known ideas and ideals, yes…! Leaders of the 'free world' have gravitated to these ideals.

Can there not be better?

Possibly… the Chinese have another variant of democracy, but that variant does have its flaws too. It compromises on freedom and that brings it several notches down in becoming a valid preference. Communism, Socialism, Monarchy, Dictatorship all have their pluses and minuses, but a combination of Democracy and Capitalism, tempered by a socialistic leaning and scientific spirit seems to be the accepted optimal solution.

As of today, the general understanding is that nations built on these principles have the highest hit rate for success in the free world. Therefore it is around these ideas that we need to build up systems that can be Dharmic - capable of delivering equitable justice to all humans.

Do we have an Indian Dharma solution?

What is that solution for a Dharmic system that would be suitable for a large diverse nation like India? Have we arrived at such a system? If so, what is that system and where have we defined it?

The base document that lays the foundation for a suitable system for modern India is the Constitution of India. It is the mother document, which lays down how the Indian collective is going to execute its nation-building and nation-running. The Constitution even lays down the process by which we can improve upon the constitution itself. It tells us how we are going to function together as a team—team India.

So let us check whether the Constitution does indeed lay the ground work for a Dharmic order.

The following things can be said about the constitution:

1. The people who drafted it were amongst the best the nation could offer. Most of them had been purified in the fire of the freedom struggle. Known to have made sacrifices, most of them were well educated and well informed about the ways of the world—and yet the

education could have been a handicap as the education was not inclusive of the traditional systems that flourished in our societies earlier.

2. The set of core ideas that the drafting committee worked upon, emerged out of the freedom struggle; these include universal adult franchise, democratic republic, separation of state and religion, federal form of government, and such other. The spirit of it was a yearning for freedom for all Indians on an equal footing.

3. When they drafted the constitution, the Constituent Assembly had many democracies to refer to - the American, the British, the Irish and the German among others. These democracies being tried and tested in those nations, the lawyers in the drafting team were able to extract best practices from the various constitutions. Importantly, they picked and chose based on what would suit our nation. In addition, they also innovated where necessary to handle a diverse nation like ours.

4. The substratum, on which the Constitution was implemented, was the colonial set up that existed prior to independence. Laws that were otherwise not scrapped or modified, continued to be in operation. Most, if not all the institutions that the colonial masters built, remained in operation in the lower levels of administration. When the legislators got into the act, they began modifying the pre-existing laws and systems in consonance with the spirit of the constitution. This entire exercise resulted in a sense of continuity; and what independence brought in was not an arbitrary implant but a transition—albeit a radical transition.

5. Even deeper in the substratum was the indigenous civilization. It is the only oldest living civilization of the world and has historical records dating back to more than 5000 years ago. It has had great traditions of learning, spirituality, trade and economics that once upon a time

were among the most advanced in the world. This ancient tradition has, over the millennia, absorbed greatly from (and given to) diverse civilizations and religions of the world. It has at its very core, the ability to recognize wisdom from wherever it is available and benefit from it.

6. Though M.K. Gandhi was not alive to give (or not give) approval for the constitution that finally was written, it can still be said that his saintly presence influenced the making of the constitution. Gandhiji's was a very influential presence even four or five decades prior to the coming of the constitution. It was in this time that the basic principles that would go into the constitution evolved. He also had a huge hand in shaping the leadership of the freedom struggle, who in turn went on to influence the Constituent Assembly. Most importantly, the Constituent Assembly went out of its way to include his vision in the directive principles of state policy in part IV of the Constitution and also in some schedules of the Constitution.

7. Another important aspect of the constitution is that the diversity of India was recognized in the drafting of the constitution in important ways:

    a. One way was the novel method of having civil codes for various communities. This, we can say, is the first step towards creating a template for a democratic world government. The other democracies had so far been designed for more or less homogenous populations. India was the first democracy that was dealing with a truly diverse population. It is apt too, because India should be the nation that shows the way to Vasudaivakutumbakam (world-is-one-family).

    b. A second way was the inclusion of a feature that is built into successful democracies already existing in the world—defenses set up against brutal majorities. Just because a certain parliament has a majority it does not mean it can do anything it wants. A modern democracy has several features to protect against this. These include the presence of two houses in the parliament, the need for more than simple majority for amending the constitution, the provision for judicial review of all laws enacted by the parliament, the provision of judicial review of executive actions and finally the articulation of the rights of minorities in the fundamental rights section of the constitution.

c. A third way is that religion has been divorced from polity by treating religion as a private affair. Religion is allowed, at the most, as a matter for a private gathering of individuals in a public space. The state as such does not profess a particular belief system, but it allows for trusts and societies that profess such faith. The treatment extended to all faiths is equal in principle.

These factors more or less indicate that the constitution lays the systemic foundation of a new age. Idealism is at its best; aiming to do justice to all Indians, treating them all as equals. It aims at setting up a collective where all Indians can prosper. It is this sentiment or spirit behind the constitution, which lays down the foundation of the new Dharma.

It is within this system—established by the constitution—that Indians have resolved to team up and try to do justice to each other. Indians will try to improve it further if it does not meet its goals.

How the Constitution has fared:

It has been seven decades since the constitution has come into force. Has it manifested the force of Dharma? Has it delivered equitably? Has it fulfilled its aim of delivering freedom in 'full measure' as was the original articulated aim?

Truly speaking, the record is mixed. India is one of the more free places in the world, but it is so free that the unscrupulous take advantage of it to harm the weak. Life and limb are safe in general, but when things go out of hand the wheels of justice move rather slowly. There seems to be more disparity rather than equity in wealth, education, welfare and rights—and this disparity is rather large. As we have reckoned in the beginning, India is languishing far behind in the platform of the world on various human development indices.

It is indeed difficult to say whether seven decades of freedom is good enough a time to have cleaned up the huge amounts of poverty in the land. The USA, France and England are leading democracies and they have had centuries to stabilize and attain their present status. Is it therefore too ambitious to expect world class results from the Indian democracy in just seven decades?

In any case, for good or for worse, no one has come up with a system that can deliver more optimally. The Chinese experiment with communism and their later addition of aspects of capitalism – thus practicing their own version of democracy does not seem to really nurture freedom. None of the presently successful nations are truly monarchies. Even Great Britain is a symbolic monarchy. Besides monarchy, dictatorship and communism, there does not seem to be any other system worth taking note of.

More or less, we can conclude that, the collective wisdom of the scientific civilization has presented Indians with a bouquet of ideas and the leaders of our freedom struggle have drawn the best from it. Considering that the constitution carries the best the free world has to offer, that it embodies a spirit of equity and justice to all, that it was set up through wide consultation and that it even offers scope for improving upon it - it does represent a yearning or stretch towards Dharma. Given the lack of anything better, it becomes evident that Dharma needs to be worked within the framework of this constitution itself. The leaders in the temporal, moral and spiritual field must resolve thus, and take the nation along that path with the Supreme Self as the highest ideal worth pursuing.

Until such a time a new and better system is invented, the system supported by the constitution is the optimal one and it needs to be pushed to its practical best. The pursuit of Dharma must imply the seeking of excellence within this framework. The various religions, guru-paramparas, and spiritual and moral lights must encourage individuals to build upon this system, so that the will of the Supreme Self is manifested in its working.

The challenges are not small. Some very crucial factors need to be dealt with urgency:

The caste issue: A very important aspect of life in India, which has not yet been resolved effectively, is the caste problem. Owing to misunderstandings about the original system and the context in which it was generated, its exterior is badly maligned and its excellent core is hardly visible. Many atrocities happen in the hinterland on the basis of caste equations and this is one area where the constitution has not delivered fully yet.

Majoritarianism: Just because someone has a majority and because this is a democracy, there is a tendency to say that 'I have the stick – so the cow is mine'. That was never the intention when Democracy was chosen. There can be majorities on various bases; Sex, language, religion, caste. So if one can work up a majority on the basis of any of these criteria, does it give that group the right to do as they please? The answer is No.

Just as traditional Indian monarchy was not the dictatorship of the King, so also Democracy is not the dictatorship of the majority. The Indian kings, the excellent ones - the gods on earth - have all been known for upholding Dharma—which encompassed the traditions of righteous rule. Likewise, the principle of majority in a democracy is just a method for taking decisions, but that decision needs to be consistent with the highest values of Vasudaivakutambakkam, Sarva Dharma Samanabhava, Universal oneness of the Supreme Self, and one divine God Head for all of humanity; in short the decision must be Dharmic. This requires that adequate checks and balances are added into a working democracy, so that it will pursue the ideal of Dharmic Governance. In summary, democracy is just a method for decision making; it is not supposed to facilitate an equivalent of a dictatorship of the majority. Democracy must be an equivalent of a Dharmic monarchy by the majority.

'Nirvana' and 'needs' facilitator: The spiritual guide must look upon the arrangement by the constitution as a system that will allow for each individual to be able to reach for the highest that a human being can attain—the promise of the goods of Nirvana. In turn, the system must look to satisfy the needs of every individual—the needs that are mentioned in hierarchy by Maslow in his famous theory. The aim should be to meet all 'needs' of all stake holders without too much enthusiasm to satisfy their 'greed' or the 'wants of blind desire'. This aspect is not yet stressed upon overtly in democracy the way it needs to be. Just as spirituality was connected with monarchy in the past, spirituality must instruct democracy to rise towards Dharma.

Religion separated from government, yet influencing character building: Kingdoms and nations worldwide have benefitted vastly from adhering to the principle of separation of religion from state. Religion must not direct what the system should be, but surely, it must direct behavior of its faithful in such a way that their contributions add up to make the present system a heaven on earth. With the adoption of the constitution, the system in India is up and running. This is what the Indian must dance with right now. The endeavor of the wise and the yogis from the various religions must be to make it work brilliantly—whatever it takes. Thought leaders, spiritual lights and Religious heads must facilitate in their followers, the ability to rise in Dharma and perform their roles in society to the pleasure of the Highest—The Supreme Self—The One that governs all of humanity.

In Summary:

The foundation for the present Dharma is not laid down by a single intellectual like it was in the case of "Manu" in his kingdom, or for that matter "Muhammed the Prophet" in Arabia or to an extent even "Chanakya" in his time and age. Instead, the present system has evolved out of the inputs of academicians, revolutionaries and suzerains from across the world. It has emerged through treaties at the international level, through the definition of Human Rights and through the work of scientists. It has taken centuries to evolve and as of today, the 'materially successful world' looks at a combination of Democracy, capitalism, Social security, MAD (Mutually Assured Destruction) dynamics and such other ideals to attain stability and prosperity in the world. Thanks to alternative thought processes that arose in the form of communism, socialism, ethnic rights, and the like, improvements have continually been made to the present system.

The system in India, with the Constitution of India at its core, tries to extract the best out of all these principles. Even so, there is no doubt that the solution worked out through the constitution is far from perfect. There is currently great disparity in justice, great amount of wretchedness (even amongst the moneyed) and atrocities are being committed against the weak. Very critical, is the fact that the current system is not moving strongly enough towards addressing the issue of the environment; and there is every reason to believe that there is an impending disaster round the corner owing to incessant environmental degradation. The Indian nation is yet to pull its weight in this sphere. All these issues need to be addressed properly within the constraints and opportunities of Democracy and capitalism.

It is possible that some perfect Dharma will emerge in the future, but in the meanwhile we have to do with Democracy and capitalism. The leader has his role cut out in reading what the Supreme Self in him wants, to then push Democracy and capitalism towards greater perfection in Dharma.

Rather than fan his desires and wants, the democratic setup under the Constitution of India must facilitate the divinity present in man.

9 AN INDIVIDUAL'S DHARMA IN THE NEW CONTEXT

It is the duty of all to support and side with Dharma. All must fight and support Dharma regardless of their personality, background, status.

----Swami Vivekananda

The all-pervading Vedic Dharma: Indians are groomed, in their living environment, by the age old system that springs out of the ancient Indian holy books – regardless of which guru-parampara or religion they follow. This ancient system is perpetuated in the traditions, beliefs and practices of the Vedic religion that forms the core, and its influence is felt in the entire nation as an integral part of life itself. It also includes the caste system which is contained in the very ethos of being Indian—the caste system permeates across most religions practiced in India. Wish hard as one might, the caste system is not going away because at the core of it is a precious jewel that is the greatest strength of the Indian civilization.

This has been dealt with in depth in the book "Rising to second Freedom: Enlightened Minds and Ignited Spirit". The reasoning there shows that hidden in this system is an opportunity, which can make this nation rise to its glory yet again; that opportunity - the precious jewel - is nothing but the awareness of the Supreme Self. Lives lived in pursuit of the Supreme Self are lived in excellence, in joy and in contentment. It is in pursuit of this alone that a society, group, tribe or clan rises to prosperity.

Understanding the Vedic pursuit of the Supreme Self:

In principle, the Vedic ideal is modelled around teams of people who, inspired with the ideal of the Supreme Self, seek to connect with this ideal through any of the yogas (Appendix D). Beyond the attainment of this highest wealth (Connect with the Supreme Self)—the civilization knows—there is nothing more to gain and nothing else matters. Thus enjoying the fruits of exalted living, they work for each other in teams that share inspired lives.

In the ideal case a broad, four-fold classification of people is done, each group's primary tasks and way of life being related to the attainment of this precious wealth.

One group is totally dedicated to learning about this precious jewel. They guide others and help shape society and its processes to facilitate acquisition of the wellness, which the precious jewel delivers. At their idealistic best, the members of this group put their egos and individual identities on the line; they deny themselves and seek mergence with the Supreme Self through comprehensively understanding all about the metaphysical and its temporal implications. They pursue the yoga of discernment.

Another group of citizens put their very lives on the line. They take up arms and go in harm's way to prevent any harm happening to the people they protect. They seek to merge with the divine by participating in the yoga of action where they seek to attain to non-actorship and hence achieve union with the Supreme Self.

A third group puts its wealth on the line. The members ensure that there is commercial activity and production happening in society. Their consumption pattern may be the same as everyone else, but it is on their initiative that a society is able to organize economic activity so that the material needs of the citizens are met and society can prosper.

The remaining citizens are involved in putting their labor on the line. They offer their services in accordance to the needs of society.

Citizens of the last two categories are primarily prescribed the yoga of devotion (or bhakti) to achieve union with the Supreme Self.

In this Vedic system the members of the various groups are given control over material and financial resources in ways that facilitate their respective roles in Dharma.

Relating the four-fold dharma with modern vocations:

The four-fold set up discussed above is ideal for a monarchy and for the uncomplicated nature of society that existed for many centuries about three thousand years ago in the Indian sub-continent. The coming of modern technology and systems today however, has lined up a complex array of professions. Each of these professions could simultaneously consist of elements from more than one of the above four categories. For example, consider the Dharma-guru who is responsible for religious instruction in the army. Though he is responsible for the spiritual health of the soldiers, he is also a soldier by profession. If he is also involved in investing his surplus funds in the share market, then three of the four basic Vedic professions (in part if not in whole) are contained in his array of duties. Similarly, other professions too can be combinations of the four basic Vedic professions. A clear cut categorization according to the old classification of professions is not as easy as during Vedic times. Indeed there are professions in modern society that more or less match the four categories of past times and therefore there are opportunities in the present system that allow for such idealism. The priestly class, Soldiers, Entrepreneurs and blue-collared employees fall broadly into the four categories. However, as we have seen, the responsibilities can span areas across these strict classes.

Must we then choose between the Vedic system and the modern systems? In other words, does it call for us to jettison the four Varna thinking and start afresh? Alternatively should we reject the modern systems and go back to the old idealism?

In truth, neither would be required. The Vedic system can still continue, nurturing those who have faith in it – much as a religion does; but it must divest itself from the political aspect in accordance with the accepted principle of separation of religion from government. At the same time, it must instruct its faithful to rise in consciousness as they endeavor to play constructive roles in the upholding of today's Dharma. In other words, just as Christianity must guide Christians, Islam guide Muslims and Sikhism guide Sikhs, so also should the Vedic 'religion' guide those who believe in it, so that the followers serve to raise the system, as envisaged by the Constitution of India, to perfection in Dharma.

Call for value based professionalism enlightened by the Dharmic impulse:

A call to Dharmic values is a joyous and contentment filled way forward, with a promise of equitable prosperity in society. This call for Dharma is not necessarily a call to bring back monarchy. It should rather be about maximizing the best that our democratic system – set up by the constitution – has to give.

How must one go about it?

The Mahabharata is an exposition built around the Dharma of soldiers. However, that does not mean the others in society did not have instructions in Dharma. Everyone had guidance on what they ought to do and what they ought not to do. For example, the queen mother had a Dharmic role, so also the sentry, the tailor, the farmer and so on. Likewise there needs to be guidance for what today's teacher, doctor, lawyer, researcher, politician, policeman, media person, house wife and so on have to do in Dharma.

Considering the above a task remains to be done—make an exhaustive list of professions that can be pursued in today's world and lay down ideals in each. This must be done by authorities in spirituality and outstandingly reputed and honorable experts in those respective professions. The society, and each individual in it, must have access to a clear vision to guide them in the pursuit of Dharmic excellence in these professions.

Religions must not divorce themselves from how their faithful participate in civil society:

Religions must instruct their followers in the sustenance of Dharma. The actions of individuals in their participation in normal civil society, definitely has an impact on their neighbor—another child of God. The performance of duties with diligence and discipline in the society helps in the sustenance of order/Dharma; and Dharma is the greatest benefactor. Righteous performance of duties is therefore pleasing to the Supreme Self (and to the Supreme Being). For this reason, religions—in keeping with their own highest spiritual goals—must guide their faithful to perform righteously in their respective contributions to society in general. Instructions by religions, in Dharmic performance of civic duties, are therefore warranted.

For example: It is not ok if someone steals and murders out in the world and comes to a temple, church, or mosque and offers a 'cut' as donation to God. Doing what displeases God on the civil side and doing what pleases God in a house of worship on the other, and then balancing the two like a mathematical equation, only leaves behind a confused individual. Such actions only serve the ego. Righteous action, in both temporal and religious duties, is of essence because the spirit matters in both spheres. Surely, one can and must separate 'religion' from polity – and that is good but that must not be interpreted to mean that 'spirituality' must be separated from polity. These are two different things and religion is not worth its salt if it does not nurture the spirituality of its faithful.

As for faithful of the religion of the Bharatas, Karma Yoga (refer Appendix D) must be re-defined in the framework of the present system. They must realize that the Supreme Self is desirous of establishing a successful system under the Constitution of India. They must therefore merge their will into the will of that noble desire that the Constitution bring prosperity for India, for all its citizens and for all children of God.

The caste plays a role in deciding Dharma:

It is pertinent to note here that the caste system is a vital clog in this setting up of standards that can meet such high idealism. While the caste system is one of the cornerstones of social design in Indian philosophy, it is the current connotations of 'Casteism' that is not desirable. Even a cursory look at the Indian society will show that it is not a question of only four castes but instead there are thousands. As analyzed in the book 'Rising to Second Freedom: Enlightened Minds and Ignited Spirit,' it is based on the family, the close ties between certain families, the education that happens from even before birth, through infancy, childhood and thereafter. It is impossible to standardize all this happening in families over geographies, over professions, over established traditions and over the passage of time. Diversity of family type - diversity of caste – is only natural. Different groups will come up with different solution arrangements for the same problem. Diversity of caste is therefore natural and a casteless society is a meaningless ideal to pursue.

In one trivial case 'casteless society' does make sense though. It is when the term 'casteless society' is used in the realm of higher consciousness. All tribes, all castes, all families, all teachers must drive their wards to understand that when it comes to consciousness, there is universal oneness across castes. When one elevates consciousness to grasp universal oneness, all groupings—including castes and gender even—become irrelevant. The call to live that high state of consciousness can be a valid call to live a 'casteless society'—in the mind and in the attitude. This apart, families will be different and castes will definitely exist just because their approaches to life will be different.

Just as organized religion is vital to the spiritual growth of the faithful, so also families and castes (groups of families) play an important role in the spiritual growth of their members. Those castes that have benefited from the yogas (refer Appendix D), including (and not only) Gyan, Bhakti and Karma Yoga, have had the benefit of excellence in their members ultimately ensuring prosperity for those families and castes. This in turn has benefitted overall Dharma. Therefore, within themselves, families and castes can lay foundations for excellence.

Dharma, as far as it is referred to at the level of doing the Will of the Supreme self, is the same for everyone. But on ground, it manifests differently for different people. Profession, religion, caste, ambient situation etc. instruct actions that each individual must take. Though a generalized broad direction can be given to large groups of individuals telling them about Dharma, it is up to each individual to find what is expected in his specific context and pursue it to the best of his ability. The family, caste and religion play an important role in facilitating this.

Example, role of sexes: Of particular importance is the role of the sexes in Dharma. The call for equality is almost a chant in the present age. There is a crucial question required to be asked here. What is it one is considering as 'Equality' here? One must first probe this. The spirit that drives man or woman from within is indeed known to be the same; physiological differences however do set males and females apart. This calls for one to consider the implications of this in the role nature meant each sex to play. A particular family or caste, guided by someone it considers most established in wisdom, may decide to divide the responsibilities in the family between the sexes in some particular way. Another family or caste, under instructions from their best guide, living in a different religious context, from a different geography, having different traditions may work out a different optimum solution. Just as diversity is ordained in dharma of individuals, different families—specific to their context—need to divide the responsibilities between the sexes in different ways. A rigid and universal standardization of roles of men and women would not make practical sense. At best, broad guidelines can be laid. One needs to recognize that the eventual separation of roles is something that characterizes castes, families, professions and individuals; they must have the flexibility to choose what suits them. What is of prime importance is whether a family or a caste is nurturing value systems that propel its members to excellence. Such excellence can only accrue in environments that nurture equity and justice amongst its members and remain mindful of matching roles to natural abilities.

Education must extend its scope to include matters of the spirit:

The teaching profession is primarily aimed at shaping minds and inculcating temporal skills. But instead of restricting itself to the three R's and possibly some Physical education, it must expand the scope to handle matters related to inculcation of a dharmic attitude in students. A contemporary educational institution must keep away from religion in accordance with the overall dharmic arrangement, but it must not keep away from spiritualism. Secular aspects of the works of the wise of the past can inspire an educational institution to raise the bar for the students. Dharma is one such secular ideal. Consider the following:

1) Excellence is related to matters of the spirit.

2) Genuine empowerment happens when the members go on to play Dharmic roles in society.

3) The true rising of a caste in society happens when, as a tribe, it builds up greater resonance with the Supreme Self.

Given these truths, an outstanding institution realizes that completeness in education is attained only when the students have learnt their lessons in this regard. Similarly, any teachers of worth, who wish to help students tap into their highest potentials, can do so only when they are able to address the student's connection to the Supreme Self. This is what distinguishes a teacher as inspirational. This is highlighted in the Mahabharata as the difference between an Acharya and a Guru. While Dhrona was an Acharya to Arjuna, Lord Krishna was the Guru. That journey from being an instructor to an inspirer is the journey every teacher must take in their own pursuit of the Teacher's Dharma. Only then can the teacher understand the Dharmic role a student would have to play in life. Only then can he guide the student along the path that leads to contentment through enacting one's Dharma. All this implies that educational institutions must innovate and facilitate gurus among teachers, to ensure that spiritual lessons relating to Dharmic performance of duties must reach their students—while at the same time keeping religion away from the curriculum.

In summary:

Having understood that the Constitution of India lays the foundation for the Dharma of today's India, it becomes necessary to design the dharma of individuals in such a way that it leads to the sustaining of the Socialistic Democratic Republic in the manner of doing justice to all Indians. Spiritual lights, religious leaders, teachers and caste leaders must all help individuals in identifying their true dharma as an integral part of the pursuit of excellence and as the path to finding fulfilment in life. They must manage to raise the standards so high as to stretch towards the idealism of the Supreme Self.

Each individual, having identified what that role is, must also realize that his role has to be played in a way that it will help him realize the Supreme Self within him. Towards this end, he must listen to the wise, seek out the best of traditions and follow the trail blazed by the best in his field. Through every action, one must aspire to attain oneness with the Supreme Will.

10 RISING WITH DHARMA: DUTY, DISCIPLINE, DIGNITY

It is impossible to find fulfilment on the path of gratifying your senses. The sooner you truly understand this, you will be on the path to liberation.

----Sirshree Tejparkhi

Practicing Dharma is the supreme method for improving the quality of our human life.

----Geshe Kelsang Gyatso

The masters only point the way. But if you meditate And follow the dharma You will free yourself from desire. 'Everything arises and passes away.' When you see this, you are above sorrow. This is the shining way.

----Gautama Buddha

Listening to the inner self and knowing the system - both are important:

As an individual, seeking to walk the path recommended by the ancient wise (the path they themselves blazed), the pursuit of Dharma is nothing but listening to one's heart, completely devoid of all ego, and completely absorbed in the present moment - alert and one with the Supreme Self. In such a state "There is no 'other'" (Sirshree). When there is no 'other', it is about the 'self' in that individual doing for 'itself' in other individuals. Acts committed by self-realized people with this understanding, even if construed as anarchic, will be in the best interest of everyone. This is what is called 'enlightened anarchy'.

However enlightened anarchies are not advisable in societies where there is a mix of realized souls and non-enlightened individuals. Systems become necessary and such systems need to be set up, sustained and continuously fine-tuned to meet the highest collective goals. Herein lies the challenge of setting up the systemic 'Dharma' that we saw earlier as one of the four important aspects of Dharma. And we saw that for Indians the constitution became the mother document for the setting up of a systemic dharma.

We have also seen that such an arrangement having been made, it enjoins duties to every individual; a task/responsibility that one needs to do in the system to ensure that the system delivers its goods to the Supreme Self. The aim should be that welfare is maximized and due justice is done to every individual.

The system having been set up and the individual having been assigned a role in it, it becomes necessary for each individual to see how their role plays out in the larger picture. Each individual must ask of themselves, 'How does my little work fit into the scheme of things at the level of the nation and humanity?' With complete awareness of this role, they must do their duty diligently and with discipline.

It therefore entails both, understanding the system and knowing from one's own heart, the Will of the Supreme Self.

Who is wise?

When one is not sure what the Will of the Supreme Self is, it is best to ask and take guidance. But who is wise?

In principle, it can just be said that where the ego dissolves, happiness grows and relationships improve – you can say a guru's influence has borne fruit. There are however, examples of people masquerading as spiritual lights. It often comes to light at a later time that their efforts are nothing more than an innovative business, using the benefits of mind science. Some of them even indulge in fraud and wickedness.

Some others work in the realm of Sattwa, mistaking it for Self-realization. There are still others who through penances, attain to great Siddhas; through the exhibition of unnatural powers so obtained, they stake claim to the right to guide. Finally, there are those who rise up in religious organizations to reach respectable heights and derive from such office a claim to wisdom. Though each religion has a Spiritual Light at its very core, these office bearers sometimes end up leading the flock astray out of a mistaken understanding of spirituality, even though their efforts may be earnest and their approach sincere.

The question therefore is who is the right one to follow?

This is one question each individual has to answer to oneself. There are pointers which one can rely on though:

- Being born to their parents, the lessons the parents give guide children along paths that require faith and trust very early in life.

- Being born in a particular family, a certain faith is inherited.

- Outstanding teachers often enter people's lives and act as guiding lights.

- The scriptures are a great source for such guidance.
- Maslow recently made an excellent investigation into the phenomenon. His book on peak and plateau experiences, based on this research, is an outstanding resource for those who are scientifically inclined. This book can only constitute the basic foundation of the argument though. It is necessary for the keen student to extrapolate from the findings and identify those that seem to enjoy these experiences—the ones who are also aware.

All these resources provide maps which individuals can use in their own spiritual journey; but each of these maps has its own opportunities and limitations—and there are no guarantees.

It is not uncommon to find Self Experienced people in this world. Maslow says that according to his research, he found that almost all those he interviewed reported having had peak or plateau experiences that are equivalent to the eastern concept of experiencing the Supreme Self. According to him, the only exceptions were those who did not want to admit to it. The challenge is elsewhere: it is not easy to find people who experience it and also 'know' that it is a spiritual experience at the same time. Even rare are those who are aware of the Spiritual Experience and manage to 'stay' in it perpetually. The Supreme Self Experience is one thing, Supreme Self Realization is another and Supreme Self Stabilization is a grade beyond that. The number of people who can be classified into the latter two categories are rather small.

"Who is the right person to follow," is not a question never asked before. One particular answer of interest came some thousands of years ago. The discussion is secular. The answer is given at the level of principles. It is from the Bhagwad Gita:

Arjuna Said:

2.54: *What is the definition, o Kesava (Krishna), of a man of steady wisdom, absorbed in contemplation? How does a man of steady wisdom talk, how does he sit and how does he walk?*

The verses 2.55 through 2.72 constitute an elaborate, principled and universal answer to this question and it is not easy to do better. For those who have no problems with referring to maps left by past travelers, this is an excellent map. (Refer Appendix E)

Guidance can be received even in the absence of spiritual masters:

It is not necessary to be discouraged if someone is averse to using metaphysical references. Guidance can be sought from purely temporal sources as well.

In order to raise one's performance at one's job to excellence, it is important to know what constitutes the best in that field. The usual term used in the present world is 'high professionalism'. Many a times the term is used to hide 'ruthlessness,' which again is not the aim as 'ruthlessness' does not harmonize with the sense of Dharma. Professionalism is about compassion, about excellence in that field; it is about doing that job diligently and maintaining high discipline while at it. As we have seen in the last chapter, it is about finding out the trails blazed by outstanding men in that field who have lived(live) sublime lives earlier—such as those that have won honor and fame for having done that particular job well. Professionalism is about living that high idealism, it is about having a great attitude while working at excellence.

Lesser Vs fulfilled lives:

Everything ultimately boils down to the quality of lives lived. Empirical observations from Spiritual masters do point out to a lower quality of life lived in the absence of the idealism that encompasses the pursuit of Dharma.

Jesus had healed many blind people and four such miracles find mention in the New Testament. A person blind by birth was cured in one go by Jesus Christ; A mud paste was applied on his eyes and he was instructed to wash it off in a particular pool and he could see. The miracle at Bethsaida on the other hand took place in two phases and it reveals Jesus Christ's sense of humor. After the first intervention, Jesus Christ asks the man, "What do you see"? And the blind man replies "I see people; they look like trees walking around." Jesus Christ works on him again and the man's sight is restored fully. To understand this one needs to look at the context. The verses in the bible where this miracle is reported, Mark 8:11 to 30, relate to the behavior of the Pharisees and of his disciples—both of who show shallowness in faith. Putting two and two together one can see that Jesus Christ is pointing out that life lived without faith is one lived without meaning. Life lived like the Pharisees who were testing him and trying to trap him or like his followers who could not see the extent of his spiritual influence, were like lives of trees walking around (kind of vegetating?). What he wanted to communicate to his disciples he made the half-blind man say; the point being that they were living listless—like trees moving around.

There are more direct messages too. Take this for instance:

For what is a man profited, if he shall gain the whole world, and lose his own soul? or what shall a man give in exchange for his soul? Matthew 16:26

In this passage it comes through that the exclusive pursuit of things of this world does not win his favor. A similar message comes to us from the Bhagwad Gita

Verses 3.16-18:

He who does not follow here this cycle thus set revolving, who leads a sinful life and delights in the senses, in vain, o Partha (Arjuna), does he live

But that person who delights only in the self, is satisfied with the self, is contented in the self alone, has no duties to perform.

He has nothing to gain by action or by inaction in this world; nor does he depend on any being for attaining his purpose.

These passages from the Bible and the Bhagvad Gita point out to, besides other things, the fact that a life lived in pursuit of things other than the Supreme Self, is not worth it.

The call in both instances is to live sublime lives. In another place, Jesus Christ says so directly: "Man does not live on bread alone but on every word that proceeds from the mouth of God" (Matthew 4:4). To really live and not exist - to have passion and not vegetate - must be the endeavor of every individual.

Those who are not well versed with—or have aversion to—matters related to the metaphysical, can make a small substitution and still benefit from this. Instead of Dharma, focus on duty: "Do your duty; be Diligent and have Discipline".

For those who know the scriptures and have faith, the call is to "Do your Dharma; be Diligent and have Discipline". They are advised to take to karma yoga (Appendix D), to rise to highest level of consciousness while they perform their acts. The usual Kama and Artha pursuits are part of the normal course; they may pursue them but with a sense of dharma and lined up for moksha in which the individual's Will merges with the Will of the Supreme Self. In such an approach there is everything to gain; a fulfilled life not lived in vain.

The lives of exalted tribes and tribesmen:

The core principle therefore, in all of this, is surrender to the divine and selfless performance of Duty. It means the surrender of the ego. Even in Christian teaching, the same point is driven home— that the only way to the Highest is that of surrender of the body (and every aspect of individuality it represents - including the ego).

Pursuing this induces great passion in life and many individuals, families, tribes, societies, nations have risen to such heights. Human History is replete with examples where, this wisdom having dawned on the people of a particular time, they rose to provide for themselves stability and peace and achieved great prosperity for their citizens.

It is strongly recommended that one must watch the motion picture 'The Last Samurai' and reflect upon the life-style of the Samurai in order to get a 'feel' of the intensity of the life of the tribe that is discussed there. The passion for living 'life' in this context is far removed from either the sedentary couch potato consumerist life style of today, or the grinding rat race for promised wealth… It is a cultural shock of sorts and therefore one may miss the point completely if not initiated into the passion and thinking of these people. It reflects the strong elements of Dharma. Surely, the passion is not far removed from the intensity of the action heroes of today… not the reel-life ones, the real-life ones. A life lived in heroism is one that allows tapping one's full potential. The lives of all known achievers in the history of mankind reflect true heroism.

The bible says, 'there is no greater gift one can give his friends, than his own life'. That is what a soldier does; when a soldier lays down his life in battle, he cannot make any use of what he will get in return. This does not make sense—except in relation to the idealism of the Supreme Self. To have lived such idealism, when they were alive and to have lived it even at the time of death, is the life of the hero.

The same applies to everyone else too. To give up one's ego and its futile pursuits; taking one's duty forward in the manner of pursuing the ideal of Nirvana, to a zone of the universal-self, is a life that mimics the life of true heroes. If that is the idealism that one lives while pursuing their profession, they would have successfully raised their job to a passion. They would move from mediocrity to inspiration and from drudgery to Dharma.

As Lord Krishna tells Arjuna in Bhagwad Gita "Take to yoga and arise" …

APPENDIX A
FOSTERING CORRECT ATTITUDE IN COMPANIES

The bigger picture is important: - "How does my little work fit into the scheme of things at the level of 'service to humanity'…?" And "there is nothing wrong in receiving a salary as is commensurate to workers in particular strata in a company… That pay must be adequate to cover the needs of the person and his family, but it is not the primary thing that drives a man's life".

The best way a company can foster excellence within itself is to make the workers responsible, let them know how they fit into the global scheme of things, make them realize that their contribution to society and to others' lives is significant—they must enlighten them about their contribution to Dharma.

The company too must stand up for it… the brand of that company must represent its great value to society and it is there that the workers in its fold will find their greatest satisfaction…

Organizational Behavior and Motivational Theory literature of this day more or less are now linking up with a basic application or practice of spirituality. Increasingly, the findings of the scientists can now be explained using the basic principles related to

'Dharma'. In a similar manner, the altruistic leaning/bent of various other modern theories too are easily explained by the principles related to Dharma. Any man of science will testify that a theory that explains a wider range of observations is likely to be more advanced.

Therefore, could we at this point conclude that what truly motivates workers is their inner nature; and that it is represented by the impellers 'Dharma' and 'moksha'? By instinct, one can tell that they do show great promise as the probable reason. The readers, of course, must continue to investigate for themselves — for in spirituality, finding proof is the student's task and it cannot be delivered from outside.

If one were to go by the great amount of stress the Indian civilization has placed in the concept of 'Dharma,' one would do well by placing faith in it. The worker indeed works best when he has risen into enacting his 'dharma' to achieve 'excellence'.

Those who are not able to gather proof for the 'Supreme Self' do not have to lose heart. In the term 'Dharma', there is a consolation prize of equal significance. There is knowledge associated with "how a radio is manufactured", but even those who learn to 'use the radio' can benefit from the most precious of its gifts. People must therefore learn to 'use' Dharma to good effect and it must begin at the individual's level – first applied to himself.

Ultimately, leaders of any rank in an organization, must realize that the values contained in Dharma must be promoted. They must encourage those under them to rise from individuality and enter excellence. They must inspire their team uphold Dharma.

Dharma in the context of Organizations' contribution to society: It is instructive to visit historic sites and take a peep into the life styles of the rich and famous of that time. Consider the Mughal Kings of Delhi; they ruled a nation about two thirds the size of today's India. The ruling class of this empire represented the cream and cherry of society during the sixteenth century (The Taj Mahal is testimony to their prosperity and status).

At Fatehpur Sikri, about 40Kms from Agra, the Mughals constructed a fort that was considered to be a kind of summer home from which they would operate at convenience. Within its walls, one comes across a monument said to be the living quarters of one of Akbar's famous ministers 'Birbal'. Akbar is considered the most prominent of the Mughals and this minister was, by far, one of the most prominent citizens of the kingdom. It hardly takes a few minutes to scan through the rooms of this monument; the entire area would probably have a floor space of about 1500 or 2000 square feet.

Pausing for a moment at this monument one could indulge in taking guesses about the arrangements in the room…. Artificial illumination, curtains, furniture, quilts and may be a 'punkah' (traditional fan) that was manually operated from outside the room… and from there mentally transport oneself to a middle class or upper-middle class family home of today. One would be surprised to note that our middle class today lives in greater material luxury than one of the top Ministers of such a vast empire.

The amenities available to common man now, were nonexistent at that time - in fact, today's middle class has it better! Birbal's house at Fatepur Sikri may only have been a summer home for the minister, but even so, the farm houses of the people of today's upper middle class would easily outdo those quarters. Today we have music and entertainment at the push of a button. You even have cool weather in the peak of summer heat if you can afford an AC. In contrast, the Mughal officials had to leave the hot climes and travel hundreds of miles to cool themselves at hill stations.

What is the reason that there is such material 'prosperity' today? Why are a great many people enjoying the comforts that even the elite of those times did not have? We owe it to the scientific civilization and the Industrial Revolution. Within that, we owe it to the R&D efforts, trade, competition, companies, workers… Clearly, if the activities that encompass the present 'economics' were not invented, the great gifts of modern civilization would not have been available…

Knowing this, any person who works in an organization must realize that they are a part of this magnificent process that is bettering the lives of humans all over the world. Their work therefore, is a gift to humanity. They are participating in the progress of human kind. Organizations therefore have a definite role in Dharma and workers in it are therefore upholding Dharma.

That gets us to an interesting question: 'Why do people work in organizations?' Definitely for salary, perks, privileges, status… but that is a matter of perspective… Are they also working for other things like upholding 'Dharma' for instance? Indeed they are…

A project manager of a company was asked about his managing director… 'Finally what is this boss of yours doing? Just making money…is he not?' The manager shook his head and said 'no… he is struggling to create a good living for those working in his factories and for their dependents.'

Here too it is a matter of perspective, but one must take note that this difference in perspective makes a great difference to one's attitude and bearing. It follows from one of the cardinal principles of mind science—that what you think, you become—if the manager's boss is actually pursuing this altruism and this is indeed what the manager perceives, then the manager too experiences the beauty of it. The manager too works with such an altruistic frame of mind… and that in turn prods him to excellence… indeed both of them, boss and project manager, do outstanding work…

All successful companies do have workers who are thus involved in the process of wealth-creation, leading to the wellbeing of a small or large portion of humanity—working for Dharma.

One may consider this a 'hypothesis'; a check with successful companies will reveal that most of them, if not all, will be churned by this spirit from within.

APPENDIX -- B
PANDIT DEENDHAYAL SEES
CONSTITUTION AS SUBSET OF DHARMA

The following is an extract from the series of lectures given by Pandit Deendhayal Upadhyaya in April 1965. One can see that he has indeed interpreted Dharma not in a limited sense of something that has to be within the confines of religion, monarchy or Hinduism. He also argues that the constitution is a subset of Dharma. One will notice that his approach is empirical. He speaks from a gut feeling as against reasoning out on the basis of core ideals or basic principles... and he is quite on the mark... clearly he is giving divine authorship to Dharma and argues that it needs to be alive and kicking and in the 'now'. The extract is being added here to support the arguments in the book and to show the general direction that Dharma truly points to...

'...On the one hand, we used the word religion as synonymous with Dharma, and on the other hand, increasing ignorance, neglect of our society and Dharma, and greater acceptance of European life, became the outstanding features of our education. As a result, all the characteristics of a narrow religion, especially as practiced in the West, were attributed automatically to the concept of Dharma also. Since in the West, injustice and atrocities were perpetrated, and bitter

conflicts and battles were fought in the name of religion, all these were listed en bloc on the debit side of Dharma. We felt that in the name of Dharma also, battles were fought. However, battles of religion and battles for Dharma are two different things. Religion means a creed or sect; it does not mean Dharma. Dharma is a very wide concept. It is concerned with all aspects of life. It sustains Society. Ever further, it sustains the whole world. That, which sustains, is Dharma.

The fundamental principles of Dharma are eternals and universal. Yet, their implementation may differ according to time, place and circumstances. It is a fact that a human being requires food for maintaining his body. However, what a particular person should eat, in how much quantity at what intervals, all these are decided according to circumstances. It is possible at times that even fasting is advisable. If a typhoid patient is given normal food, the consequences may be disastrous. For such a person, keeping away from food is necessary. Similarly, the principles of Dharma have to be adapted to changing times and place.

Some rules are temporary and others are valid for longer periods. There are some rules regulating our conduct at this meeting. One of the rules is that I speak and you listen with attention. If in contravention of this rule, you start conversing with one another or addressing the gathering at the same time, then there will be disorder; our work will not progress: the meeting will not be sustained. It can be said that you have not observed your Dharma. Thus it is our Dharma that we observed the rules by which the meeting proceeds smoothly. But this rule is applicable only as long as this meeting lasts. If after the meeting is over, even when you reach home, you continue to observe this rule and do not speak, a different problem will arise. Your family might have to call in a doctor. At home, the rules suitable there will have to be observed. The complete treatise on the rules in general and their philosophical basis is the meaning of Dharma. These rules cannot be arbitrary. They should be such as to sustain and further existence and progress of the entity which they serve. At the same time they should be in agreement with and supplementary to the larger framework of Dharma of which they form a part. For instance, when we form a registered society, we have the right to frame the rules and regulations, but these cannot be contradictory to the constitution of the society. The constitution itself cannot violate the Societies Registration Act. The act has to be within the provision of the Constitution of the country. In other words, the Constitution of the country is a fundamental document which governs the formulation of all acts in the country. In Germany the constitution is known as the "Basic Law".

Is the Constitution too, not subject to some principles of more fundamental nature? Or is it a product of any arbitrary decisions of the constituent assembly? On serious consideration, it will be clear that even the Constitution has to follow certain basic principles of Nature. Constitution is for sustaining the nation. If instead it is instrumental in its deterioration, then it must be pronounced improper. It must be amended. The amendment is also not solely dependent on majority opinion. Now-a-days the majority is much talked of. Is the majority capable of doing anything and everything? Is the action of the majority always just and proper? No. In the West, the king used to be the sovereign. Thereafter when royalty was deprived of its so-called divine rights, sovereignty was proclaimed to be with the people. Here in Our country neither the kings, nor the people, nor the parliament have had absolute sovereignty. Parliament cannot legislate arbitrarily.

It is said about the British parliament that it is sovereign and can do anything. They say that "British Parliament can do everything except making a woman a man and vice versa." But is it possible for the parliament to legislate that every Englishman must walk on his head? It is not possible. Can they pass an act that everyone in England must present himself before the local authority once every day? They cannot. England has no written Constitution. They regard tradition highly. But their traditions too have undergone change. What is the basis for making changes in their traditions? Whichever tradition proved an obstacle in the progress of England, was discarded. Those which were helpful in the progress were consolidated.

The traditions are respected everywhere, just as in England. We have a written constitution, but even this written constitution cannot go contrary to the traditions of this country. In as much as it does go contrary to our traditions, it is not fulfilling Dharma. That Constitution which sustains the nation is in tune with Dharma. Dharma sustains the nation. Hence we have always given primary importance to Dharma, which is considered sovereign. All other entities, institutions or authorities derive their power from Dharma and are subordinate to it...'

From the above passage what seems missing is the declaration that Dharma is the will of the Universal Soul; for the Universal Soul is timeless, it sustains the nations, it sustains humanity; constitutions of nations are to be made in harmony with the same. The Universal Soul is the same within all of us. Clearly Pandit Deendhayal Upadhyaya is either avoiding the mention of the core principle - and taking the argument forward on the basis of facts that are commonly argued upon in intellectual circles, or he is moving inwards from the periphery. That is to say, through his lifelong efforts—yogic practices— and the associated learning, he is able to churn out the essence of the notion of Dharma by merely focusing on the world that is perceptible to the senses. In either case, he is quite on the mark.

Following is a passage again from the same work 'Integral Humanism' in which he seeks to reveal how Manu was eventually handed the task of laying down the Dharma of his times... In other words, Manu was being asked to lay down the constitution for that time...

...Later on interruption and disorganization came into existence. Greed and anger dominated. Dharma was on the decline and the rule "might is right" prevailed. The Rishis were perturbed over the developments. They all went to Brahma to seek counsel, Brahma gave them a treatise on "Law and the Functions of the State", which he had himself written. At the same time, he asked Manu to become the first King. Manu declined saying that a king will have to punish other persons, put them in jail and so on; he was not prepared to commit all these sins. There upon Brahma said, 'Your actions in the capacity of king will not constitute sin, as long as they are aimed at securing conditions under which the society can live peacefully and according to Dharma. This will be your duty, your Dharma. Not only that but you will also have a share of the Karma of your subjects, whereby you will gain Dharma considerably if your subjects maintain conduct according to Dharma.'...

Those who are wary of the use of the icons of Hinduism like Brahma for instance, can simply represent this to mean that a deep process of prayer, meditation and discussion unravelled an 'Inner Voice' which said Manu had to persist with laying down the rules regardless...

APPENDIX – C
SECULARISM IN CONSTITUTION IS TODAY'S YUGA DHARMA: K SUBRAMANYAM

This article is able to interpret the eternal principle of Dharma in the context of the present age. The point is to see the principle contained in it. The author is able to draw the relationship between upholding Dharma and upholding the rule-of-law and is thereby able to reveal the intent of the Supreme Self in today's context. The article is able to bring out how those desirous of rising their routine works to the level of consciousness of Dharma can do so even in the context of modern jobs, tasks and responsibilities.

NEED TO UPHOLD DHARMA   ----
K. Subrahmanyam

(As it appeared in THE SPEAKING TREE: Times of India; 3rd Feb 2011)

Hindu tradition is based not on acceptance of particular gods, dogmas, revelations and religious structures but on reverence for Dharma which is the rule of law and the ethics of the age. In the Hindu way of life there are no God- or Prophet-given laws. Dharma is not immutable but is liable to change to be in consonance with changing times — hence, the concept of yuga dharma. Today's ethics, formulated by the constitution, is secularism — that is the yuga dharma. Violators of it cannot be considered Hindus; they can only be looked upon as enemies of the Hindu way of life.

The true Hindu way of life is in danger today but not from those who follow other religions. It is threatened by those who want to imitate others and abandon its essence, because they have misinterpreted it through the prism of dogmatic faiths. For those who assert 'Brahmasmi'' and 'Tattvamasi', it does not matter if the temple at the birthplace of Rama comes up a few years or a few decades later, if it comes up at all.

Why is Rama the most popular of all the nine avatars? Because he was a Maryada Purusha, who gave Ram Rajya (good governance) and defended Dharma (rule of law). Rama cannot be venerated by those who transgress Dharma by killing innocents. A way of life which highlights the birth and death cycle, allows one the freedom to worship God in any form or not to worship at all, proclaims the cosmic universality with its Advaita cannot be reconciled with the killing of innocents.

The Hindu way of life will survive because it is the natural, free, inquiring way. The reverence for life, which is the essence of birth and death cycle, the worship of Ishta devatas and the ability to see God in all things living and non-living, has to be restored. The temptation to imitate others by trying to straitjacket the free Hindu way of life into structural frameworks must be resisted. Dharma — the rule of law — must be restored. Ram Rajya — good governance — should be established and nourished. The Hindu way of life is not the same as accepting an organised religion. Therefore, this way of life can be propagated, cherished and practised without having to come into conflict with other religions. Comparing the Hindu way of life with other religions is like comparing apples and oranges. The Hindu way of life is the essence of secularism. Its thought processes and philosophical reflections are meant to be observed privately; in public, Dharma, the rule of law, has to be respected.

Recently, the prime minister referred to two kinds of Hinduism — one of Vivekananda and the other of the self-styled "Hindu" extremists. The latter is in the same class as the extremist clergy of religions. There is no difference between those Hindu extremists and the fundamentalist clergy of Semitic religions. Part of the problem is that the Hindu way of life has not been explained to our children as a secular way of life and that it is not the practising of a religion as understood elsewhere in the world.

The writer (January 19, 1929-February 2, 2011) was a strategic affairs analyst and consultant editor with the TOI. This article is abridged from Dharma Was Killed in Gujarat Violence' published on April 4, 2002.

www.speakingtree.in

APPENDIX D
KARMA YOGA

http://sinduland.blogspot.com/2011/12/karma-yoga.html

This is a read and chew, chew, chew, chew, kind of paper… It may require the kind of inquiry one takes up in order to understand Quantum Mechanics. Be that as it may, it still gives a how-to-do step-by-step guidance to an important touchstone of Indian Spirituality.

"Take up to Yoga and arise" was the concise message that Lord Krishna had for a dejected Arjuna at the battle field. So what is Yoga and specifically 'Karma Yoga'? And how does it make one 'rise'? Can it really pitch me to excellence? Can it really unleash my highest potentials?

For those that are unfamiliar with the basic precepts of the Hindu spiritual studies, it will suffice at this point to consider the following as a postulate:

"Being human in our approach is considered to be a resultant of 'ignorance' where we wrongly attribute a personality to the body-mind mechanism. The dawning of an unshakable realization that this presumption is an error; and there by discovering and surrendering everything to the 'True Self' that lies deeper within, is considered 'enlightenment' or 'nirwana' or 'Self realization' or 'wisdom'."

This would mean that spiritual explorers are advised to seek to transcend from ignorance to self-realization and for that they must take to any possible 'exercise' that will help them make progress in their journey. This is where the various 'yoga' come into play; Karm Yoga is one of them.

'Yoga' can be defined as that mental-spiritual posturing (which may also consist of posturing in the physical world), as a result of which ignorance is dispelled and Self-realization is achieved. Through this yogic process, a human-in-ignorance at the beginning, sheds the 'personality' and what is left, is a mind-body mechanism in which the ignorance is dispelled; the 'mind' or 'personality' becomes silent, and the 'Self realizes itself'. Yoga is therefore the 'exercise' that catalyzes transcendence in an ignorant individual.

Karma Yoga: When talking of Karma Yoga it is usual for people to quote one passage from the 'Bhagwad Gita' which goes like this...

"Established in yoga, O Dhananjaya (Arjuna), perform actions, giving up attachment, and unconcerned as to success or failure: this equanimity is called yoga" 3:48

Truly speaking, this is just the punch line; karma yoga, as such, consists of taking to certain mental postures that are comprehensively described in the verses of the Gita ranging from 3:39 to 3:53

The following verse begins this narration:

"The (requisite) mental attitude towards the self has been just taught to you, now hear about it in respect of the way of action (Karma-Yoga), being endowed with which (attitude), O Partha, you will get rid of the bondage of actions". 3:39

Note how the 'yoga' is referred to as a 'mental attitude' and also note how the consequence is referred to as the point where one gets 'rid of bondage of actions'

Studying the essence of the passages that follow, let us consider the steps that are declared as constituting Karma Yoga...

Assurance that there is nothing to lose:
'You will get rid of the bondage of actions...'
'There is no waste of undertaking...'
'There is no chance of incurring sin...'
'It is a religion, and even a bit of it saves you from great danger.'

It has to do with one pointed determination and focus on the Lord:
In this exercise (yoga), your mind achieves one pointed determination. The alternate to this is an irresolute thought process which is multi-branched and endless or infinite... This alternate path does not lead to excellence and it does not lead to one-point concentration in God

Beware of delusion and of wanting enjoyments of fruits of action; especially when people speak flowery words to that effect from the scriptures:
You will come across people who will regard Heaven as their highest goal, they will be enamored by the panegyric statements in the scriptures and of sayings of spiritual masters and will assert that there is nothing else (higher than this). They will quote flowery and familiar words from the Great texts, prescribing numerous kind of rites that produce birth, actions and their results as a means for enjoying power. However, they will be dull-witted and full of desires and attached to enjoyment and power. Their minds will be carried away by the flowery words... and though they speak of the

scriptures they do not have one-pointed determination that can lead to concentration in the Lord. Beware of this pitfall

What must your understanding be in respect of the volumes of knowledge in the scriptures?

Know that these verses from the scriptures are like small reservoirs and their purpose is served by a large lake… When transcendence is attained in an individual, it forms a huge lake and can serve almost the same purpose as these numerous reservoirs. So be reassured that all that is in the Vedas is taken care of in the path of he that takes to Karma Yoga…

Do the following and you need not bother anymore about the lessons that come from all the scriptures…

As a summary of all that the scriptures teach you, know that the Vedas elaborate on the three gunas (Sattwa, Rajas and Thamas). All that you need to do is to rise above these three gunas and always be established in goodness (sattwa), regardless of whether you the individual is blessed with acquisition, preservation and self-possessed… This should the substratum when you take to Karma Yoga...

The attitude when approaching action:
a) you have rights to work but never claim the result
b) as such do not make the result as the motivation for your action
c) and at the same time do not interpret this as you needing to be attached to inaction; Established in yoga perform actions giving up attachment—unconcerned as to success or failure…

This equanimity is Yoga

Take refuge in wisdom:
Work done with desire is far inferior to that done with wisdom

Those who are impelled by desire are miserable
Endowed with wisdom one gets rid of both good and evil
Therefore take to Yoga

Yoga is skill in work

There is no fear of evil from those who truly practice karma yoga
Endowed with wisdom
Giving up the fruit resulting from action,
Attaining self-realization
And freed from bondage of birth
Surely
They go to the abode which is free from evil

The transition happens in due course and the final point is when understanding rests in the Supreme Self:
When your understanding will get beyond the maze of delusion, then you will have attained the difference to what is to be heard and what is heard
When your understanding, (now) perplexed by hearing, will rest in Samadhi (the Lord), unwavering and steady - then you shall attain yoga.

THEREFORE
Yoga leads to one point concentration in the lord and there is nothing to lose
Yogic Transcendence results in a lake where Vedic sayings are small reservoirs
Rights for actions—yes: Rights over results—no: Motivated by results—no:
Equanimity is Yoga
Refuge in Yoga is refuge in wisdom
Yoga is skill in work
Yoga is an abode which is free from evil

When Understanding rests in Samadhi you shall attain yoga

Having understood the steps involved one must take up his duties in the world with this attitude in mind... he will eventually move into the realm of the 'Heroes'... into the 'zone'... into the world of the charmed and charismatic...

APPENDIX E
WHO IS WISE?

Following is a non-sectarian view on the qualities of a self-realized Soul. These verses are taken from the Bhagwad Gita (Swami Vireshwarananda translation). These are authoritative words, succinctly put, that describe the nature of one that is wise.

2.54: *What is the definition, o Kesava (Krishna), of a man of steady wisdom, absorbed in contemplation? How does a man of steady wisdom talk, how does he sit and how does he walk?*

The verses 2.55 through 2.72 constitute an elaborate principled secular answer to this question

55. *When a man gives up all desires of the mind, o Partha, and himself delights in his Self, then he is said to be a man of steady wisdom.*

56. *He is unperturbed in misery and free from desires amidst pleasures, who is devoid of all attachment, fear and anger—that sage is said to be of steady wisdom.*

57. *He who is free from affection everywhere, and who getting whatever good or evils neither welcomes nor hates them, has steady wisdom.*

58. *When he completely withdraws his senses from the sense-objects, even as a tortoise its limbs, (then) his wisdom is steady.*

59. *From an abstemious embodied being (man) sense objects fall off, but not the relish (for them); but even this relish of the man of steady wisdom ceases when that Supreme Being is realized.*

60. *The turbulent senses, O son of Kunti, forcibly lead astray the mind of even the struggling wise person.*

61. *Controlling all these (senses), the self-controlled one should sit meditating on Me. Verily, his wisdom is steady, whose senses are under control.*

62-63. *For a person thinking of the sense-objects there grows an attachment for them; from attachment arises desire, from desire results anger, from anger results delusion, from delusion results confusion of memory, from confusion of memory results destruction of intelligence and from destruction of intelligence he perishes.*

64. *But that person of controlled self, who moves about amidst sense-objects with the senses governed by the self and free from attachment and aversion,--he attains serenity.*

65. *When this serenity is attained, there results the destruction of all his misery. Verily, the wisdom of the serene-minded one gets steady soon.*

66. *For the uncontrolled person there is no knowledge, nor is there meditation for him; and for the unmeditative person there is no peace, and for one bereft of peace how can there be happiness?*

67. *Whichever of the wandering senses the mind follows, that one carries away his wisdom as the wind a ship on the sea.*

68. *Therefore, O mighty-armed one, he whose senses are well controlled for their objects, has steady wisdom.*

69. *That which to all creatures is night, is where the man of self-control is wide awake, and that in which (all) creatures are wide awake is night to the sage who sees.*

70. *He attains peace into whom all sense-objects enter, even as rivers enter an ocean that is unaffected through being ever filled, and not one who is desirous of enjoyments.*

71. *That person who giving up all sense-objects, goes about unattached, devoid of the idea of ownership and free from egoism—he attains peace.*

72. *This is the Brahmi state, O Partha (Arjuna), attaining it one is not (again) deluded; one who rests in it, even at the time of death, attains Nirvana in Brahman.*

APPENDIX F

INSIGHTS FROM A. C. BHAKTIVEDANTA SWAMI PRABHUPADA

Swami Srila Prabhupada is the preceptor and founder of the ISCON movement. He identifies the universal oneness as the "Krishna consciousness". Following are some of his observations on various occasions that throw light on the subject of our discussion and we can see in the arguments that he talks about obedience to God as being of central importance. This is Dharma...

The following excerpt from a lecture made in 1967 shows that in his view Hinduism is not a religion and therefore cannot be classified in a set whose other elements are "Christian" "Buddhistism" or "Islam"

> *Actually, "Hindu," THERE IS NO SUCH WORD AS "HINDU" RELIGION. We don't find in the Vedic scripture. Hindu religion... Hindu*

> *religion is a modern term given by the foreigners. Actually the Indians, bharatiya, they, their religion is varnasrama-dharma, religion of four castes and four spiritual orders, four spiritual orders and four social orders. The persons who follow these four orders of social status and four orders of spiritual advancement, they are called varnasrama. SO HINDU RELIGION IS A MISCALCULATION.*

(CC Lecture - NY 11/1/67)

In the following excerpt Swami Prabhupada argues that once a system or 'religion' as he calls it has been constituted by none less than the 'Highest Consciousness' which he usually refers with the term 'Krisna Consciousness'. Then it is all about obedience to that divine will and to the system constituted by the divine will.

> *Vedic religion means varnasrama-dharma. That is... Krsna says, God says, catur-varnyam maya srstam [Bg. 4.13]. So that is, what is called, obligatory. Just like law is obligatory. You cannot say that "I don't take this law." No. You have to take it if you want to have a happy. You cannot become outlaw. Then you'll not be happy. You'll be punished. So God says maya srstam. "It is given by Me." So how we can deny it? And that is religion.*

Conv. - Vrindavan 28/6/76

In another instance, in a conversation with Dr. Kneupper, Swami Prabhupada brings out that there is a common inspiration. He calls it as 'veda' and insists it does not signify anything that divides people. It is just plain knowledge. He talks about knowledge of God and about what He wants—implying Dharma.

> *Everyone should understand God and the relationship with God and act accordingly. Then it is perfect*

religion. And if there is no conception of God, no carrying out order of the God, that is not religion. That is cheating. But generally they do not accept God—still, he is stamping himself that "I am Hindu," "I am Muslim," "I am Christian." He has no idea what is God, how to abide by His order, and they are fighting that "I am Christian and you are Hindu. Therefore we must fight." This is going on. Nobody understands what is God. Pseudo religion. Practically there is no religion. If there is no government—you make your law; I make my law—then how there will be peace? That is the position. They do not understand what is God, and "I am Christian" or "Hindu" or "Mohammedan, so let us fight." That's all...

Vedic knowledge means to understand God. Vedais ca sarvair aham eva vedyam [Bg. 15.15]. So anyone who tries to understand God, he is in the Vedic line. Veda means knowledge, so as you get the stock of knowledge, that is called Vedas. But as soon as we say Vedas, they think it is Hindu. Mathematics is a science. So any scientific man will accept mathematics. Where is the question of Hindu mathematics? Gold is gold. If it is in the hand of Hindu, it is Hindu gold? Hindu, Muslim gold? Gold is gold. When we give the Vedic knowledge, they think it is Hindu idea.

Room Conv. –Vrindavana 6/11/76

ABOUT THE AUTHOR

Mr. Nixon Fernando is an academic and a post graduate in the three disciplines of Physics, Government and Business Administration. He is also Author of four books dealing with leadership, science and spirituality, and National development. He served as a lecturer at the NDA for 10 years from 1996 to 2007 (where he received Commandant's commendation for excellence in service). He was also a lecturer at the Great Lakes Institute of Management for six years; and Course Head (Program Head) at the MIT school of Government for one year. He has been in close association with Mr. TN Seshan, legendary, former CEC of India and served as his research assistant towards an autobiographical work.

An ardent student of the Bhagwad Gita and the New Testament, he considers Sirshree Tejparkhiji of the Tej Gyan Foundation as his Guru. Having just turned 50 he has spent more than 25 years researching socio-political-spiritual-economic solutions for India.

www.ingramcontent.com/pod-product-compliance
Lightning Source LLC
LaVergne TN
LVHW031243190726
843493LV00010B/2991